down by the riverside

down by the riverside
a brief history of | BAPTIST FAITH

Everett C. Goodwin

Published with funding from the
American Baptist Historical Society

JUDSON PRESS ■ VALLEY FORGE

down by the riverside
a brief history of | BAPTIST FAITH

Library of Congress Cataloging-in-Publication Data
Goodwin, Everett C.
Down by the riverside: a brief history of Baptist faith / Everett C. Goodwin.
    p. cm.
Includes bibliographical references.
ISBN 0-8170-1400-4 (pbk. : alk. paper)
1. Baptists—Doctrines. 2. Baptists—History. I. Title.

BX6331.3 .G66 2002
286—dc21   2002141558

Printed in the U.S.A.

10 09 08 07 06 05 04 03 02
10 9 8 7 6 5 4 3 2 1

to my mother,

PAULINE FREEMAN GOODWIN

A lifelong Baptist, the wife of one Baptist minister and mother of another, she has lived the high calling of being a Baptist. From her childhood church not far from Nebraska's Platte River, to participation in denominational leadership, she has experienced the foibles of Baptists in general and of Baptist preachers in particular. She has loved them anyway.

contents

preface

Given the title and content of this book, you most likely picked it up because you want to know more about who Baptists are and what they believe. Perhaps you have encountered Baptists in reading or engaged them in conversation. You might be new to the Christian faith or attending a Baptist church for the first time. Maybe you have been a part of the Baptist community of faith for a longer period of time but have never given much thought to what makes Baptists different from other Christians.

There is also the possibility that you are a seasoned Baptist who is interested in learning what another Baptist is saying about what it means to be Baptist. For as all seasoned Baptists know, contemporary Baptists are not in full agreement about which Baptist principles are essential and how they should be understood and applied today.

This book is intended especially for those with little previous knowledge about Baptists. No prerequisite resource is required. I have tried to define carefully all terms that may be new to those unfamiliar with the church or with Baptist life. But though written for beginners, the content goes beyond the bare basics. More than just providing dates, names, and places, I have attempted to draw connections and provide interpretation so that readers might gain a sense of what it means to be Baptist.

An important part of knowing who Baptists are is understanding who Baptists have been and where they came from. As a historian interested in Baptists, I am inclined to emphasize the importance of understanding the past. But although this book includes information about Baptist history, ultimately it is not a history book. Thus, while a historical style dominates the presentation of the information, the historical material is greatly condensed. For the sake of those who would like to know more, I have included recommended readings as an appendix to the book.

My hope is to promote an understanding of the Baptist heritage, a heritage that I have been pleased to receive and am proud to represent.

For the sake of brevity I have elected to use notes sparingly in presenting the material in this book. However, I want to make clear that little of the specific information in this volume is original, but rather is gratefully restated or reinterpreted from the works of a great many others. A number of interpretive directions and statements, on the other hand, are my own, and I bear responsibility for them.

It is not propriety but genuine pleasure for me to acknowledge those whose work has especially informed this book. They include many of the eminent Baptist historians and writers. From a previous era, the writings of Winthrop S. Hudson, Norman Maring, and particularly Robert Torbet were steady guides in shaping these pages. William Estep was most helpful in reviewing the influences that shaped the earliest Baptists, and Walter Shurden's concise summary views of historic Baptist principles and beliefs were invaluable. I am greatly indebted to Gordon S. Wood, William G. McLoughlin, and Edwin S.

Gaustad, all of whom inspired me with their scholarship, and who in different times and places have provided much-needed personal encouragement for this and other projects.

I take special pleasure in continuing a relationship with Judson Press in the publication of this work. As that press continues in a direct line from the earlier and historic American Baptist Publication Society, a consciousness of the great cloud of Baptist witnesses—and critics—is acute. I am grateful to Randy Frame of Judson Press, whose encouragement and patience were critical in nurturing the completion of this project, and Rebecca Irwin-Diehl, also of Judson Press, whose editorial assistance helped complete it. Deborah van Broekhoven of the American Baptist Historical Society played an important part in conceptualizing the idea for this volume and provided helpful insights and encouragement along the way. My daughter, Leah, provided helpful insights and suggestions at several stages of development.

Writing is an individual task, but it takes its toll on the community from which the writer draws his or her strength. I am particularly grateful, therefore, to the congregation of the Scarsdale Community Baptist Church for encouraging the diversion of some of my time and energy to this work, and to my family, who overlooked much in order that it might be accomplished. My most important acknowledgment, for the necessary life perspective for this work, I have stated in the dedication.

Everett C. Goodwin

section one

baptist beginnings

chapter 1

baptists at a glance

Gonna lay down my burden, down by the riverside.
—Traditional Spiritual

For nearly four hundred years, people called Baptists have gathered for baptism down by the riversides of their experience. Sometimes they have gathered by actual flowing rivers or on the shores of ponds, lakes, or oceans. In later times they have laid down their burdens in the purified, temperature-controlled waters of the baptistries in their church buildings. Their baptisms have symbolized a changed life and a desire to walk more closely with the God who, they believe, has saved and redeemed them and who calls them to worthy service in a new kingdom both on earth and in heaven.

The Baptist venture began in England and soon extended to the North American continent with, at most, a few dozen despised and outcast adherents among the early British and European settlers. Today, Baptists constitute a global community of Christian faith and witness. In some parts of the world Baptists are perceived as a sect. In some places they are considered to be a threat to peace and stability, often because they advocate principles of freedom in faith and of democracy in organizational development—principles that threaten authoritarian or totalitarian leadership. In some places Baptists represent the political or social elites; in other places, oppressed minorities.

Baptists have enjoyed particular prominence in North America, especially the United States, where Baptists represent the largest Christian expression of faith outside the Roman Catholic Church. One single Baptist organization, the Southern Baptist Convention, constitutes the nation's largest Protestant denomination. In the United States, Baptists are prominently represented in Congress and can claim several United States presidents—among them Harry Truman, Jimmy Carter, and Bill Clinton—as Baptists in practice or in heritage.

Through thousands of churches with millions of members, Baptists reflect a vital, continuing community of faith. In addition, Baptists have contributed greatly to some of the underlying principles by which North American culture endures and prospers. And even while they reflect much of the change and transition occurring in our own time, Baptists continue to hold that certain principles and beliefs are enduring, and these they strive to maintain.

Baptist principles of belief and practice are critical for Baptist self-understanding and growth. Some Christian denominations set forth their essential principles of faith and practice in creeds and catechisms, typically to be memorized by all participants. In contrast, Baptist individualism and freedom have caused less specific definition of Baptist faith.

A Baptist generally believes in the power and authority of the Bible and often has experienced some form of spiritual awakening that he or she identifies as a moment of conversion or confession of faith. Baptists love to sing; there is an informal catalog of hymns and songs well known to Baptists. And Baptists uniformly believe that they are called to be God's witnesses and agents in transforming the world, although often they disagree about the specific nature of the desired transformation and the particular means of achieving it.

Baptists believe in mission, and despite differences of opinion about many other matters, they frequently find their most important unity in developing and supporting mission programs ranging from evangelism and preaching to the establishment of hospitals, educational institutions, and advocacy organizations for political, social, and personal reform. In organizational matters, whether in a small village church in Maine or in central Africa, or in a large multiministry institution such as New York City's Riverside Church or Abyssinian Baptist Church, Baptists believe that the Holy Spirit may be relied upon to guide and direct a congregation to make its decisions in conformity to God's will. Thus, Baptists are democratic in process. And they are often, therefore, noisy and messy in procedure.

Historically, Baptists have been more of a movement than an established organization. But it is a movement of highly individualistic members. This is partly because Baptists had no single leader, no matriarch or patriarch, no Martin Luther to stake out a broad confession of faith, no John Calvin to define a theology by which all belief is to be measured. One result is that there has been no single standard to which individual Baptists or Baptist organizations could turn for specific guidance. Baptists have been blessed with a remarkable number of notable leaders, pastors, and visionaries, but none has given rise to a universal theological formula or specific plan of action.

Baptist leaders seem to have emerged in times of crisis or in response to particular need. Adoniram Judson, an idealistic young man in New England's Congregational churches, first responded to a call to mission for that denomination, but soon determined that the Baptist way was more biblically accurate than his Congregational heritage. He spent a lifetime defining Baptist missions beyond American shores. Walter Rauschen-busch, a German Baptist shaped by his early ministry to immigrants in New York City's Hell's Kitchen, first became a faithful shepherd to his flock. Then, having understood a link between the gospel and social change, he shaped a significant ministry as a seminary professor and writer teaching a social, transforming gospel. Martin Luther King Jr., raised under the tutelage of his father's ministry, became a pastor too, and looking beyond the pews of his own sanctuary, determined to follow a call to address the needs of a whole people.

In short, Baptist leaders have responded to needs, have articulated visions, and have been architects of ecclesiological plans. Remarkable and memorable men and women have appeared among them, but none has created a "system" that endured. None has become a "name" to which all others pay obeisance. Unlike Methodists, for example, who historically look to John Wesley as the shaper of their practice of faith, Baptists have no single progenitor. Instead, they have followed a variety of leaders.

With this quick impression of the general features of Baptist identity in mind, we move to an overview of Baptist history.

chapter 2

baptist beginnings

In the early sixteenth century, a spirit of great change engulfed religious practices and institutions in Europe. What had been a single, outwardly united church with its spiritual and administrative headquarters in Rome suddenly came under severe criticism by many reformers. These reformers had widely differing experiences and viewpoints. Martin Luther, a Roman Catholic monastic and priest, is symbolically understood to be the progenitor of what is now called the "Reformation." Soon, many other reformers, among them John Knox and John Calvin, joined in offering corrective views and plans for churches of greater discipline, faith, and vitality.

Even prior to Luther and his contemporaries, however, many individuals and groups had misgivings about practices of worship and belief in the Roman church. Some of these early reformers and prophets, such as Jan Hus and Balthasar Hübmaier, professed beliefs and principles that eventually would be practiced by Baptists. And some of these early groups of Christian reformers, such as the Waldensians, Moravians, and Hutterites, conducted their lives in spiritual community in ways that some later Baptists adopted.

During the Reformation, additional reformers emerged, believing that the original reformers had not gone far enough. Among these reformers was a group loosely called "Anabaptists." This term, which literally means "rebaptizers," was used negatively to identify those who were perceived to have gone too far in rejecting the traditional ways of faith and worship and too far in creating a spirit of commonality and equality among followers.

Anabaptist practices of faith centered on personal regeneration, discipline, and the guidance of the Holy Spirit. Many believed that this kind of religion encouraged heresy and chaos, and therefore was suspect and dangerous. Even such reformers as Luther, Calvin, and Knox, who themselves were considered radical by the established church structures, viewed Anabaptists with discomfort and alarm.[1]

Amid this religious ferment of the sixteenth century, it is difficult to know for certain who influenced whom. However, Baptists, especially in America, most directly trace their origins to a small group of "Separatists" who were part of the continuing Reformation in England. Separatists, similar to their radical counterparts on the continent in Europe, concluded that the traditional church was hopelessly corrupt. Therefore, they believed, a true church had to be created apart from the historic church structure.

Separatists were subject to extreme disapproval and oppression by the authorities of the established church in England. These church authorities had the support of the government behind them to enforce conformity to official belief and church practices. Many, including the great writer John Bunyan, were imprisoned or otherwise punished for their beliefs or for their refusal to adhere to the established ways. Others were deprived of their rights, privileges, or possessions.

One group of Separatists, a congregation led by John Smyth and assisted by a wealthy and influential member of the group, Thomas Helwys, fled to Holland in 1607 to seek relief from oppression. Holland was relatively tolerant toward refugees, particularly refugees from religious persecution.

In Holland, Smyth and his companions encountered a group of moderate Mennonites, and under their influence, he professed to become an Anabaptist. Anabaptists insisted on a conscious act of baptism by adults as a sign of their regeneration, and the Mennonites in particular organized their congregations with a strong sense of discipline and most often were characterized by a commitment to peace. Smyth was particularly convinced by their view on "believer's baptism." He determined to organize his followers on the basis of personal confessions of faith and believer's baptism.

Smyth rejected the Calvinist views held by most Separatists. That is, instead of believing in a process of election or foreordination of believers, he maintained that Christ died for all and that all who trusted in him would be saved. In addition, he adopted many of the Mennonite teachings on the importance of discipleship, religious liberty, the governance of the church, and the separation of church and state.

Smyth and the congregation that he led particularly emphasized adult (believer's) baptism. Smyth believed that the baptism practiced on newborn infants was of no spiritual value. He therefore first baptized himself by pouring water over his head, and then proceeded to baptize about forty other members of the church, including Helwys. Although baptism by immersion had been practiced by the early church, and some radical reformers had advocated it, this practice was not common at the time.

Smyth died in August of 1612. Soon thereafter, Helwys led the remaining ten members of the original congregation back to England, where, just outside the city walls of London, they gathered a church at Spitalfield. It was noted in public records as the first Baptist church in England.

In founding their new church in England, the congregation established an important principle. Smyth had believed that a magistrate (government officer) could not be a member of the church. Helwys and his group rejected this view, asserting that as long as a magistrate was committed to Christ and followed his Lord in baptism, he would be permitted church membership, with the same privileges and responsibilities as others.

This was a critical decision. To have excluded magistrates or others based on their social or political role, as some more radical reformers advocated, probably would have had the effect of making Baptists a strictly sectarian and marginal group and would have severely limited their development. Helwys and this small congregation were also willing to take an oath of allegiance to the king and were willing to serve in defense of the nation.

These principles made these early Baptists marginally more acceptable to the authorities, and likewise made them suspect in the view of more radical reformers. But Helwys insisted that the jurisdiction of the crown (the government) was limited to civil matters, and that any attempt to order the affairs of the church, including the official Church of England, were in error. He articulately argued this position in a little book entitled *The Mistery of*

Iniquity, for which he was arrested and imprisoned in Newgate Prison.[2] There, less than three years later, Helwys died. His death, perceived as martyrdom, ultimately helped to establish as a Baptist principle the strict separation between church and state.

One of Helwys's colleagues, John Murton, became his successor. Murton had returned to England with Helwys, and like Helwys, he had published books on religious liberty and also had been imprisoned. He survived for ten years, however, and from prison he helped to plant several churches by his writings, conversations, and spiritual leadership. By the time of his death in 1630, there were eight Baptist congregations established in and around London. These churches, along with others that they established and influenced, set the first principles of Baptist church life, based on regenerate membership, strict separation of church and state, congregational governance for church affairs, and a strong commitment to publicly accepting the consequences of their belief.

The Baptist churches established in and around London and influenced by the Smyth and Helwys church came to be known as "General Baptists." They continued to reject Calvinist influences, believing that Christ had died for all and not just an elect number. During the same period, another kind of Baptist church also emerged in London, whose members came to be called "Particular Baptists."

Particular Baptists maintained not only that baptism by the established church was invalid, but also that baptism by sprinkling or pouring of water was incorrect. Particular Baptists thus began the practice of baptism by full immersion. By 1644 there were seven churches reflecting these views and practicing baptism in this manner. It was also in 1644 that Particular Baptists created the *First London Confession*, which expressed a Calvinist theology, supported baptism by immersion, and affirmed the principle of religious liberty.[3]

By the end of the seventeenth century, the word *Baptist* had come into general use to refer to those who insisted on believer's baptism, despite other differences among them. Like the Puritans, early Baptists struggled to create a "pure" church without forsaking involvement in the world around them. They especially upheld the principle of religious liberty, both as a hard-learned lesson from their own experience and as an article of belief from their faith, according to which any spiritual experience, to be valid, had to be voluntary.

Early Baptists were committed to independence during a time when both governments and religious organizations with vested interests in maintaining control sought to assert their authority. Therefore, from an early moment in their development, many Baptists sought to practice their faith in places where they would not be impeded or punished. Some of them sought their future in the "New World."

notes

1. See William R. Estep, *The Anabaptist Story: An Introduction to Sixteenth-Century Anabaptism,* 3d ed. (Grand Rapids: Eerdmans, 1996); idem, "Sixteenth-Century Anabaptism and the Puritan Connection: Reflections on Baptist Origins," in *Mennonites and Baptists: A Continuing Conversation,* ed. Paul Toews (Winnipeg: Kindred Press, 1993).

2. Thomas Helwys, *The Mistery of Iniquity* (1612; reprint, London: Kingsgate Press, 1935).

3. For additional information and texts of the various Baptist confessions of faith, see William L. Lumpkin, ed., *Baptist Confessions of Faith* (Philadelphia: Judson Press, 1959).

chapter 3

baptist origins in america

People came to the New World for different reasons, but many were looking for the freedom to practice their faith and to establish their churches as they believed God had directed them. This was especially true of the Puritans, who first came to the colony of Massachusetts and then quickly spread to colonies along the northern Atlantic seaboard.

In the seventeenth century, *Puritan* was a word that loosely described people who had an earnest faith and a profound conviction that the established Church of England was in desperate need of reform. The Puritans who came to America in the 1600s were seeking the freedom to establish a communal society and a practice of faith based on biblical principles as they understood them.

The Puritans were interested in establishing their churches and community as they desired, but were not equally willing to tolerate deviation from their own vision. In fact, it was quite the opposite: Puritans tended to believe that the only possible chance for spiritual as well as civic success in the New World lay in their ability to create churches and communities that were built on common foundations and principles. They believed that these principles were revealed in the Bible, and they were convinced that their spiritual and community leaders were the right people to interpret and to implement them.

Inevitably, this created tension between the majority and any minority or individual who might understand things differently. From their earliest years, Baptists were chief among those who saw things differently. The story of Baptist beginnings in the New World is in part the story of a clash between Puritan and Baptist ideals.

The person who, both as a personality and as a symbol, best stands as a beginning reference point for Baptists in America is Roger Williams.[1] Born in London in 1604, Williams was a small child when Smyth and Helwys took their little congregation to Holland, and was a young adult when Helwys returned to England and began to establish Baptist roots in London. Williams was well educated and trained to be a priest in the Church of England, but he was influenced by the Puritan movement. In 1631 he moved, with his wife, Mary, to Boston. Soon thereafter he became "teaching pastor" of the Puritan church in Salem, Massachusetts.

Williams soon discovered that he had serious disagreement with some of what the Puritan leaders of Massachusetts practiced or advocated. These disagreements centered on the relationship between the church and the state.

The Puritans believed that, under God's direction, they were creating a "New Israel." They sought to institute religious laws as civil laws, to maintain God's order in social affairs, and they directed that churches and the legislative government should work hand in hand to accomplish this goal. They believed that only members of Puritan churches were fit to be full citizens in their communities. They maintained that the Puritan clergy had been ordained to determine right belief and understanding, and that the civil authorities had been ordained to structure and monitor right behavior.

Williams, however, maintained that the civil authorities had no jurisdiction over the consciences, including the religious beliefs, of citizens. The Puritans, in contrast, believed that to tolerate such a view would erode the authority by which the clergy and magistrates ruled.

In addition, Williams exasperated Massachusetts authorities—especially John Cotton, the powerful and persuasive pastor of the First (Puritan-Congregational) Church of Boston—because of his views on how Native Americans should be treated. Cotton argued that the Massachusetts Bay Colony was the equivalent of the New Israel, and the Puritans were God's chosen people, fleeing oppression and pursuing a new and promised land that God had ordained for them. In Cotton's view, the Native American people were the same as the biblical Amalekites.[2] Therefore, killing these native people and possessing their land was justified and consistent with God's purpose.

Williams believed that the New Israel was to be populated by the regenerate faithful and therefore could not be established on racial or national grounds. He also claimed that these natives were objects of God's mercy and, in fact, persons with whom the English settlers were supposed to share the gospel. Williams claimed further that the settlers were morally wrong in not paying the native people for the land they had taken to settle. In short, Williams threatened the authority of the establishment.

Williams was tried for his beliefs in 1635, and when convicted he was banished from the colony. An appeal at first gained Williams a delay, but in January of 1636 he learned of a plan to seize him and send him back to England. He left immediately, enduring the hazards of winter weather over land and sea, and, along with four companions who joined him, he fled to what is now Providence, Rhode Island.

In his new location, Williams practiced his own policies and paid the native people for the land on which he settled. Moreover, he dealt with them forthrightly and as equals. He refrained from any attempt to make converts among them unless they invited him to do so. By developing a relationship of trust, Williams was able to contribute to early European understanding of the people who first inhabited New England, and in 1643, during a voyage back to England, he wrote a book, *A Key into the Language of American Indians.*[3]

Rhode Island, which Williams was instrumental in founding, soon became a haven for dissenters, including Quakers and Baptists, Jews, and others who were not welcome in Massachusetts. Because of its openness and tolerance, it stood for everything that the Puritan leaders despised. In Providence, Williams joined with several others of Baptist belief to establish what became the first Baptist church in the colonies (today identified as the First Baptist Church in America). However, Williams did not remain long in the fellowship of that congregation. Although it is probably inaccurate to define Williams as a Baptist for any length of time, at least in institutional terms, his principles and example, particularly regarding matters of conscience and the strict separation of church and state, became strong foundations upon which Baptists soon built their common commitment.

Across Narragansett Bay from Providence lay two other communities that established religious liberty: Portsmouth and Newport. Both were influenced by the leadership of a quite different personality, Dr. John Clarke. Like Williams, Clarke had left London to pursue religious liberty and, like Williams, discovered that the Puritans of Massachusetts were unyielding on points of liberty dear to him. He was driven out of the Massachusetts colony in 1638 and eventually purchased Aquidneck Island from the native people. He renamed it Rhode Island. Clarke supported himself by practicing medicine, but when a Baptist church was formed in Newport, he became its pastor.

The law codes of these Rhode Island settlements ordered that "none be accounted a delinquent for doctrine, provided that it be not directly repugnant to the government or laws established." In other words, religious belief was none of the government's business. Rhode Island's commitment to personal liberty, and especially to freedom of conscience, soon caused the other New England colonies to be wary of the little colony and its inhabitants—the "cesspool of New England," as one colonist described it.

Occasionally, Rhode Island's citizens were harassed when they visited Massachusetts. In 1651 Clarke and two other Baptists were arrested for preaching against infant baptism. They were imprisoned in Boston. One of the men received thirty lashes with a three-corded whip—a punishment that sometimes was fatal. Clarke was fined twenty pounds—nearly half a year's salary. Later, Clarke wrote of this experience in his treatise *Ill News from New England*, which, along with Roger Williams's *Bloody Tenet of*

Persecution, strongly and passionately advocated liberty of conscience at a time when it clearly was a minority position.[4]

By the end of the seventeenth century, there were only about ten Baptist churches in all of New England, with a total of about three hundred members. Baptists did not flourish in the region, partly because of the consistent persecution they suffered. By the time that increased toleration allowed Baptists to enjoy greater freedom, their identification as being among the lower social classes of people kept them from gaining significant acceptance by their neighbors and fellow citizens. They also suffered from a practical economic disadvantage: even when growing toleration allowed for freedom, Baptists were forced to pay taxes for the support of the established Puritan or Congregational churches. It would not be until the middle of the eighteenth century that Baptists would enjoy a surge of growth in New England, as a result of the religious renewal in several colonies called the "Great Awakening."

notes
1. See Edwin S. Gaustad, *Liberty of Conscience: Roger Williams in America* (Valley Forge, Pa.: Judson Press, 1999). For a readable fictional autobiographical account of Williams's experience, see Mary Lee Settle, *I, Roger Williams* (New York: W. W. Norton & Co., 2001).
2. The Amalekites, according to Genesis 36:15-16, were descendants of Amalek, grandson of Esau. The Amalekites inhabited territory assigned to Israel and Judah. The Amalekites attacked Israel on its wilderness journeys from Egypt, as described in Exodus 17:8-16, and antipathy marked their continuing relationship. See also Judges 6:1-6; 1 Samuel 30:1-20; 2 Samuel 8:12; 1 Chronicles 4:43; 18:11.
3. See Gaustad, *Liberty of Conscience,* 28–30.
4. For a sense of the faith and activity of these early Baptists, and an understanding of Obadiah Holmes in particular, see Edwin S. Gaustad, ed., *Baptist Piety: The Last Will and Testimony of Obadiah Holmes* (Valley Forge, Pa.: Judson Press, 1994). For the specific incident involving Clarke and Holmes, see pp. 22–32.

section two

baptist foundations and growth

chapter 4

foundations of baptist organization

Despite their early weakness, or perhaps because of it, Baptists in Rhode Island and southeastern Massachusetts began to organize. In 1670 four Rhode Island churches united in a yearly meeting and established a tradition of sending elders and messengers to fulfill a defined purpose of "setting in order the things that are wanting" in the churches and to solve "any difficulties that might arise." By 1729 this association embraced thirteen churches, including five or six in Massachusetts, Connecticut, and New York.

The first lasting center of Baptist organizational growth in North America, however, was in the vicinity of Philadelphia. One reason is that Pennsylvania, along with its neighbor colony New Jersey, offered a greater degree of religious liberty than anywhere except Rhode Island. In Pennsylvania, William Penn had sought a charter of government that overtly emphasized religious freedom. Penn, a Quaker, sought to benefit and encourage his own Quaker practices. Quakers themselves had endured enough persecution both in England and in the colonies to want no part of it.

In New Jersey, the proprietors had a less spiritual purpose in mind: they speculated that religious liberty would enable them to attract immigrants of all beliefs and backgrounds and thereby help to populate their colony. Baptists began to flourish in both places, but in the Philadelphia area especially they were strengthened from an early date because they recognized the benefits of working together.

A Baptist church was established at Cold Spring as early as 1684, just two years after William Penn arrived with his settlers. In 1688 a church later known as the Pennepek Church was begun by Elias Keach. Keach did not limit his parish to a village or small area, but instead extended it to include a "circuit" of congregations meeting in Chester (Pennsylvania), Trenton (New Jersey), and several other locations. In the spring and fall, the members of these distant congregations met at the Pennepek Church for worship, baptism, and the Lord's Supper. This practice diminished as membership in the more distant congregations increased and as members objected to the difficulty of travel.

This model of extended parish connections encouraged a universal commitment to joint meetings for the purposes of baptism, inspiration, and discussion of common concerns, and for the ordination of ministers. Soon, a tradition of quarterly meetings developed. Then, in 1707, five churches fixed the annual meeting as an "association" of messengers who were authorized by their respective churches to "meditate and execute designs of public good." The churches included at least as many from New Jersey as from Pennsylvania, but the annual meeting became known as the "Philadelphia Baptist Association."

In the South, the Baptist movement was established and strengthened by a steady migration of New England Baptists. Eventually, Baptist churches everywhere began to form regional associations and gatherings. The idea of an "association" proved to be a seminal one, not only influencing later Baptist organizational development, but also ultimately serving as a model for secular organizations, political party development, and charitable and educational organizations.

Baptist churches jealously protected the spirit of independence for both churches and individuals. Therefore, association decisions were always regarded as advisory. Nevertheless, over time, churches came to trust the spiritual wisdom and practical effectiveness of association decisions.

Baptist strength increased significantly in the middle of the eighteenth century as a result of a great religious revival that engulfed the entire east coast of the continent. The spirited revivalism of this broad religious movement created disabling controversies within New England's Congregational Order, among Presbyterians, and within the Anglican Church over matters of worship and church order. It did not create such problems for Baptists, however, and in fact propelled them to greater growth and personal commitment. In many places, Baptists received new members not only from those recently converted to Christian faith, but also from those who had grown frustrated with established churches that were resistant to the new "enthusiastic" worship styles the movement encouraged and who desired a different style of church participation as a result of their new faith perspective.

The tireless leadership of several strong Baptist personalities advanced Baptist interests and concerns and kept Baptists in communication.[1] Baptist practice and perspectives, especially ideas of participatory governance and independent thinking, were well suited to the era of the American Revolution and early national political consciousness in the new United States.

The populist spirit of the period of revival became part of a more general movement that culminated in the development of democratic ideals and aspirations. These in turn came to focus on that singular event of the eighteenth century, the American Revolution. Baptists were not generally in visible leadership in this political expression of the massive changes taking place in American culture. Only one of the signers of the *Declaration of Independence,* for example, was a Baptist: John Hart, a prosperous farmer from Hopewell, New Jersey. When the question of independence was brought forward, Hart voted for it. His visible leadership of the colonial causes against the British rulers eventually cost him his health, wealth, and worldly security. He died before the Revolutionary War ended.

Despite a paucity of visible national leadership in politics, Baptists exercised a great influence in the shape of both religion and politics of the latter part of the eighteenth century. This was due largely to a remarkable man, Isaac Backus, who, more than any other, helped to shape Baptist concepts of church life and organization, and whose perseverance enabled Baptists to achieve their most significant goal: freedom from the restrictions imposed by a state church and from the taxation imposed to support it.

Due to the influence of Backus and others, Massachusetts, in 1728, began passing a series of laws that had the effect of granting the rights of "dissenters." Religious groups, such as Baptists, Anglicans, and Quakers, could gain tax exemption from supporting the established Congregational churches by filing petitions for relief. Since Baptists were eager to find a place of respect and acceptability, many, if not most, were encouraged and even satisfied by these changes. Although the requirement to "register" and confess a dissenting belief might seem to have cast them in a second-class status, it seemed to many a reasonable compromise. For a few, though, it was unacceptable.

As the colonies moved toward what eventually became war against Britain, established leaders naturally were eager to solidify support. This worked to the advantage of Baptists, most of whom were strong supporters of the Revolution. At times, the British authorities had seemed to be the Baptists' only protection from the oppression of colonial leaders. Realizing this political advantage, Backus became an effective lobbyist in presenting Baptist concerns to the Continental Congresses and later to the Constitutional Convention. Such efforts resulted in establishing religious freedom in the Constitution of the United States.

In the South, Baptists had been comparatively weak and disorganized prior to the Great Awakening. However, propelled in part by the spiritual zeal of the time, a former Connecticut Separate Baptist, Shubael Stearns, led a remarkable period of growth among Baptists. Stearns had migrated south as an itinerant preacher in 1755 and settled in Sandy Creek, North Carolina. In a short time he gathered a number of converts, organized several churches, and established the Sandy Creek Association with churches from Virginia to South Carolina.

Stearns's fierce Separate principles highlighted one difference between the new and vigorous tradition of Separate Baptists and the older, more established "Regular Baptists" of Virginia and the Carolinas. Specifically, the Separate Baptists would not subscribe to the Philadelphia Confession. The matter was not really dissent from the doctrines stated in the Confession; rather, it was a matter of principle that faith must be grounded in Scripture, not on statements crafted by others.

In resolving this difference, the Baptists in the area developed a compromise that created a model that served Baptists well for the next two centuries. It was a compromise that established a clear purpose in unity but avoided any agreement on external authority. In that spirit, the Philadelphia Confession was adopted in 1787 as an expression of unity among these Baptists, but with a clear understanding that the Confession would not usurp a "tyrannical power over the consciences of any." By that means, they agreed on important matters of doctrine, such as salvation by Christ and free and unmerited grace, yet left it to individuals and congregations how to interpret and practice the particulars that the doctrines implied.

Although by the period of the American Revolution, Baptists were not a large group, they had experienced remarkable growth and possessed a revitalized energy. Rising from the few hundred Baptists at the beginning of the eighteenth century, by 1780 the single Philadelphia Association had become twelve associations in the colonies, and by 1790 there were thirty-five. By 1791 there were 564 Baptist ministers, 748 churches, and, by best estimates, over sixty thousand members.

Although their freedom was still restricted and their energies

compressed by laws that, in all but the Middle Colonies, supported state churches, Baptists possessed a revitalized sense of
belief and a dawning sense of mission. By the time that Connecticut disestablished its church in 1818, and Massachusetts
followed in the same course in 1833, Baptists had established an
effective voluntary organizational style and were creating institutions to support their activities. The Baptist movement
already was being carried into the new territories of the West
and the South, where eventually they would develop their great-
est strength and strongest work.

notes

1. As we will see later, Isaac Backus in New England and John Leland in Virginia
were assiduous in representing Baptist concerns about freedom and in shaping
Baptist consciousness.

chapter 5

from organization
to mission

As the new American nation moved into the nineteenth century, its energies were focused on expanding into new territory. Baptist energies were focused on expanding and developing organizations and institutions that would encourage their growth. Baptists in the nineteenth century had a robust sense of destiny that led to the establishment of new churches, schools, and institutions. During this time, missions emerged both as a rallying point for unity and as a basis for fundraising. By the mid-1800s it became clear that while Baptists might be united in spirit, they were destined to be divided into a variety of structures and organizations.

The current of Baptist individualism flowed into the new century with considerable force. By mid-century it was articulated with eloquence and with the authority of hallowed tradition by Francis Wayland, who was president of the Baptists' first and then most recognized university: Brown University. The New Hampshire Confession of Faith, popularized by the American Baptist Publication Society (founded in 1824 as the Baptist General Tract Society), championed the individualist perspective in many ways, including the omission of any reference to the idea of a church universal in its texts.

In addition to this individualism, however, the spirit of cooperation first expressed in the earlier associational style of the Philadelphia Association continued to represent the Baptist mainstream. Yet it had been greatly modified by the growth of evangelicalism, an outgrowth of the revivalist style. Evangelicalism emphasized the importance of a "conversion experience," and it was often characterized by a more emotional style of worship. As with other church denominations or organizations, Baptist associations and their agendas were shaped by evangelical styles of worship and outreach. By the end of the nineteenth century, the theology and practice of most Baptists were essentially evangelical.

In the South, the spirit of evangelicalism and individualism so infused the spread of the Baptist movement that evangelicalism, increasingly fusing with the central tenets of Southern cultural identity, became the defining characteristic of Baptist churches. In fact, it became common in the South to refer to any church that was evangelical in nature as Baptist, with the exception of Methodist churches, whose strong central authority preserved for them a separate identity. A similar pattern developed in portions of the Midwest and the West.

By the close of the nineteenth century, the defining Baptist characteristics were freedom, independence, and individualism. In many respects, Baptist emphases constituted a considerable gift to American religious understanding. The development of strong local congregational control advocating intensely personal freedom in matters of doctrine helped to shape a uniquely American style of religious expression.

However, these same characteristics made it difficult for Baptists to create or maintain a common corporate core or a unifying sense of institutional tradition. Individualism and evangelicalism most frequently considered institutional development to be secondary to primary purposes of conversion and growth. Evangelicalism also carried with it a deep mistrust and fear of any organization or structure that might seek to limit its impulse. Thus, it was difficult for Baptists to gather and to exercise the cooperation and authority necessary to guide and direct their common purposes.

Missions, however, was one area where Baptists succeeded in both the vision and implementation of a powerful common cause. The emphasis on missions later became so prominent among Baptists that it is important to understand that, among early Baptists, missions was a vague concept at best.

We see an early glimpse of the Baptist vision for missions in the call of an English missionary named William Carey. Carey was a cobbler who was essentially self-taught in the Bible and theology. At a meeting in 1791 in Northampton, England, Carey raised the question of whether churches had done all that they should to convert the "heathen nations." Dr. John Ryland, chair of the session, reportedly gave Carey's question a tart response: "Young man, sit down; when God pleases to convert the heathen world, he will do it without your help or mine either."[1] Ryland's response reflected the prevailing Particular Baptist view that God neither needed nor wanted human help in converting sinners, and that an attempt to convert others was not only an unacceptable method of faith expression, but it was also a challenge to God's authority and plan.

Early Baptist fervor was not based on zeal to convert to Christianity those who were without belief. Its purpose instead was to convince those who were already Christian that they ought to confess their belief and be baptized as an expression of their commitment in following God's will for them. So when Carey raised his question about the "heathen nations" of the world, he was raising a whole new and radical challenge. As he saw it, it was a "missed opportunity." And it was one that the evangelical dynamic ultimately adapted to readily and with great vigor.

Carey persisted in his question and ultimately gained the support of Andrew Fuller, another prominent Baptist leader. Fuller, moved by Carey's commitment and persistence, formulated a proposal that "a plan be prepared . . . for forming a Baptist Society for Propagating the Gospel Among the Heathens." Carey's zeal, combined with the credibility and leadership of Fuller, were, in effect, almost solely responsible for the development of the Baptist mission impulse.

Carey's dream to be the first missionary sent out by this society was fulfilled. But Carey was not the first Baptist sent out as a missionary from one place to another. In North America, George Lisle, a freed slave, went from Georgia to Jamaica at least fifteen years before Carey sailed for Serampore. Lisle was, in fact, emancipated by his owner for the specific purpose of preaching the gospel. He established a church in Savannah, Georgia, but during the Revolutionary War, following his former owner's death, his freedom was contested. Ultimately, he indentured himself to a British army officer who took him to Jamaica.

Before he left, he converted Andrew Bryan, another African American, who then became the pastor of the church that Lisle had established in Savannah. Subsequently, the Savannah church flourished and sent out pastors and leaders to start other churches. In Jamaica, Lisle worked off his indenture, and in the meantime he started a free school and mission work in rural areas, baptizing over five hundred persons in about an eight-year period. In 1789 Lisle and his congregation bought land in the city of Kingston, Jamaica, and built a Baptist chapel there. Soon thereafter he heard that a Baptist mission society had been established in England under Carey's leadership, and he sent appeals to that organization that they might send missionaries to Jamaica.

It is in this process of appeal to a society for help in evangelism and missions, small though it was, that the organizing and unifying process of Baptists had its birth. The British mission society was essentially a board comprised of representatives (mostly pastors) from several British churches. Their role was to establish policy and to raise funds for sending and supporting missionaries. With an appeal from George Lisle for their response to an island culture in a far-off part of the world, the vision for global missions among Baptists was forming.

Limited resources among British Baptists constained rapid expansion, but development of this model was effective in establishing a "denominational" identity for Baptists. It developed further in the response of the American Adoniram Judson to serve as a missionary and in the support of Baptists in North America who saw in Judson's efforts a noble cause worthy of support by all.

notes
1. Warren Mild, *The Story of American Baptists: The Role of a Remnant* (Valley Forge, Pa.: Judson Press, 1976), 25.

chapter 6

the birth of an american baptist mission enterprise

The experience of Adoniram Judson and his supporters represented the spiritual of awakening and the spiritual "enthusiasm" that characterized the new American nation. In the early 1800s religious revivals were again popular, especially in the frontier areas of Kentucky and Tennessee. Churches also were growing and developing in cities and towns of the East. Evangelicals expressed a new vitality in the founding of colleges and schools to advance the gospel among young people. Several young men, including Judson and his classmate Luther Rice, grew to maturity in this context. They longed for a vocation through which to express their faith and ambitions.

Judson was the product of a traditional New England Congregational education. Having attended Brown University and Andover Theological Seminary, he was ordained as a Congregational minister. He and several of his classmates determined to be sent as missionaries to Asia. In 1812 he and his wife, Ann, and several others sailed from Salem, Massachusetts, with their destination being Calcutta, India. They had received financial support from the Congregational board for foreign missions.

For Baptists, the Judson voyage was one that seemed later to parallel the transformation of Paul on the Damascus road. For while on the long voyage, Judson occupied himself with a task that he had begun several years earlier in theological school: his own translation of the New Testament from Greek to English. He struggled especially with the issue of baptism. His translation convinced him that valid baptism had to follow conversion. Furthermore, since the New Testament description of baptism placed it in the context of a river, he concluded that it had to be done by immersion. By the end of the voyage he was thoroughly convinced of the Baptist way. He and Ann, along with several others of the group, including Luther Rice, were baptized and declared themselves to be Baptists.

Soon after arriving in India, they resigned from the Congregational service and sent letters to Baptist leaders to see whether new support might be organized. "We are confirmed Baptists," wrote Ann Judson, "not because we wanted to be, but because truth compelled us to be. We have endeavored to count the cost, and be prepared for the many severe trials resulting from this change of sentiment. We anticipate the loss of reputation, and of the affection and esteem of many of our American friends."

The ultimate success of their appeal was aided by Ann Judson's winsome style, and by the reality that Adoniram Judson and, even more, Luther Rice were known as "stars" among the constellation of the young generation of recent seminary graduates. The high regard and visibility of Rice and the Judsons no doubt caused consternation among their supporting Congregational associates when, following their voyage to India, their change of belief became known.

At that time, English activity in India was under the control of the East India Company, a private mercantile company with a charter and strong support from the British government. This company feared that missionaries, or any others not under their influence, might disrupt their hegemony and control. The company had successfully delayed first Carey, and later the Judsons, in obtaining transportation to India or permission to stay there. As the Judson party had no legal standing in British-controlled India, they were forced to move on to Burma.

In the meantime, however, Luther Rice became ill, and it seemed wise for him to return home. He was deeply disappointed, but this would be regarded later as a fortuitous turn of events. He returned to the United States for medical treatment, and while he was there, he raised support for the Judsons' work in Burma. Over the next two decades, Rice and the Judsons forged a "bicontinental" partnership. Their common vision was to make missions a vital force among Baptists in America.

Beginning in Boston, Rice traveled tirelessly up and down the Eastern seaboard, spending time especially in Philadelphia, Washington, and the Carolinas. His mission was the same in each location: to preach a gospel that inevitably came to focus on the centrality of missions, to encourage local churches and individuals to give money for the support of missions, and to encourage young men to enter the mission field. By force of persuasion he recruited new leaders among Baptists. By the same force of persuasion in addition to his mastery of the art we now call "networking," in his pursuit of mission support, he helped to define the first organizational ties that led to denominational identity and purpose among Baptists.

In the course of a visit to Richmond, Virginia, in 1813, Rice made an impassioned appeal at a citywide meeting of Baptists at the First Baptist Church. The congregation on that day was large and, by the customs of that time, made up of white participants seated on the main floor and black persons, many of whom were slaves, seated in the galleries. In the gallery was a young slave named Lott Carey. Rice's preaching stirred this young man, and he formed a vision of his own to send missionaries to Liberia in West Africa.

Lott Carey was befriended by a young white man who taught him to read, and soon he was licensed to preach. He worked in a tobacco warehouse, where he was allowed to gather up small bits of tobacco remnants for his own use. He accumulated enough by diligent collection of these shards that he raised $850, an astonishing sum, with which he purchased freedom for himself and for his children.

In 1815 Carey participated in founding the African Missionary Society of Richmond. Within four years this society raised $700 to send missionaries to the new colony of Liberia. In Liberia, Carey established the First Baptist Church in Monrovia, and later he rose to prominence in the colony and served in the government. The strong missionary impulse and example of Lott Carey and, before him, George Lisle, inspired others and soon served as a point of denominational unity among African American Baptists.

Following the request from the Judson party for support, Baptists in Boston had organized the "Baptist Society for the Propagation of the Gospel in India and Other Foreign Parts" in 1813. Then, in 1814 Baptists and Baptist associations throughout the country by mutual consent called for a convention to meet in Philadelphia for the purpose of establishing a national missionary society, which ultimately was named the "General Missionary Convention of the Baptist Denomination in the United States for Foreign Missions." Soon, however, the popular name for the organization became the "Triennial Convention," as its meetings were held every three years. In that development, Baptist organizational life took a decisive step toward definition.

The convention board appointed Luther Rice as its first missionary, and he was directed to continue his promotional activities on behalf of mission support. At this first meeting, the Judsons also were appointed as missionaries on behalf of the convention, with instructions to establish work in Burma.

The new mission enterprise was well received. By 1815 Luther Rice reported that most of the 115 associations of Baptists supported the convention's work. This kind of cooperative effort likely helped to lay the groundwork for the establishment of a great many more Baptist organizations, including dozens of Baptist schools, colleges, hospitals, and other institutions for human betterment. It also may well have served as an example for broader ecumenical organization in the period, represented by organizations such as the American Education Society (1815), the American Bible Society (1826), the Sunday School Union (1824), the American Tract Society (1825), the American Home Missionary Society (1826), and the American Peace Society (1828), all of which were independent, interdenominational organizations that included strong Baptist participation through churches, individuals, or in a few cases, whole associations.

chapter 7

obstacles to baptist unity and mission

The creation of the Triennial Convention was a high point for Baptist success, communication, enthusiasm, and purpose. Nevertheless, Baptists faced many internal challenges, the biggest of which was an "antimissionary" movement, which was strong mainly in the South and the West. While many Baptists supported missions, other Baptists objected, replicating the original response to Carey's vision that it was an affront to God to attempt to determine who was saved and who was not. Underlying some of the opposition to missions was hostility toward Native Americans. This was a period in which settlers of European background threatened ancient customs and social patterns of the people they called "American Indians." As a result, settlers of European background in some cases had been subjected to cruel treatment. Those who lived in fear of Native Americans did not want to consider them as candidates for missionary outreach.

Often, the same groups that opposed mission efforts also opposed the establishment of Sunday schools, theological seminaries, and other attempts to educate or elevate lay and clergy abilities. At the heart of much of their concern was resistance to any effort that might threaten an absolute sense of equality or that might lead to "centralized authority."

Other developments in the nineteenth century served to discredit Baptists. One such development was "Millerism," named after New York Baptist minister William Miller. Based on computations and theories of his own devising, Miller calculated that Jesus would return to begin his millennial rule on October 22, 1844. He attracted wide audiences from among Baptists, as well as Christians from other backgrounds. When Jesus did not appear on the date predicted, not only was Miller personally discredited, but also were Baptists in general.

A second theological movement, popularly known as "Landmarkism," emerged in the South, led by two prominent ministers, James R. Graves and J. M. Pendelton. Intent on restoring practices of the early church among Baptists, they began with the assumption that the early church was Baptist. Proponents of Landmarkism refused to recognize for Baptist church membership those who had been baptized by non-Baptist pastors or leaders. They opposed the exchange of pulpits between Baptists and ministers of other churches, and they prohibited Baptists from participating in the observance of the Lord's Supper in any church other than their own.

In addition, Landmarkism taught that only members of the local church were truly members of the same "body." In its most extreme form, Landmarkism insisted that the only true membership was that accomplished by baptism in the local congregation to which the person aspired to belong, and that only members of a local church could be truly in fellowship with one another. Needless to say, such views did not encourage Baptist cooperation with Christians of other denominations. Landmarkism also impeded relationships and common causes among Baptists.

It was, however, the growing need to confront the issue of slavery and the ultimate outbreak of the American Civil War that most undercut early Baptist unity and enthusiasm and shaped the nature of Baptist relationships and organizations for the future.

To their credit, Baptists, along with other Christian groups, especially Mennonites, Quakers, and some New England Congregationalists, had opposed slavery in the eighteenth and early nineteenth centuries. And, especially in the aftermath of the Great Awakening, when humanitarian concerns had been heightened, Baptists had joined in concern about the plight of all people working in servitude, especially Africans. Furthermore, in the revivalistic movements that also followed the Great Awakening, Baptists, as well as Presbyterians and Methodists, had worked to gain members specifically among Africans in America and had received them into their churches. Opposition to slavery was not a sentiment confined to the North. For example, the Ketockton Association in Virginia had, in 1787, "determined that hereditary slavery was a breach of the divine law."

Yet many other Baptists, like much of the nation, found it difficult to deal forthrightly with the problem of slavery. Desiring to preserve peace and harmony, many churches and associations chose not to deal with the problem in the official proceedings of their organizations. In 1805, in Kentucky's Elkhorn Association, for example, ministers were urged not to address the issue of slavery, because it was a political subject. A great many Baptist ministers and lay leaders were involved, formally and informally, in challenging slavery, but organizationally, Baptists did not develop a clear and unified record in opposing it.

Although every state in the Union, especially in the older and more developed areas, North and South, was implicated in the development, encouragement, or economic benefit of slavery, the issue was most sharply drawn in the South. In South Carolina, for example, by some estimates approximately one-third of Baptist laymen and two-fifths of Baptist ministers were slaveholders in the latter part of the eighteenth century.

In Philadelphia in 1820 a church proposed that the Philadelphia Baptist Association call a national meeting to consider a plan for the emancipation of slaves among Baptists. The answer was that it was "inexpedient to enter on such business at this time."[1] In general, the majority of Baptists were reluctant to formally approach the issue out of a desire to preserve unity and because there were slaveholders or those involved in slave-related business in a great many Baptist congregations. Also, some cited the Baptist principle of the separation of church and state as a reason not to get involved in political affairs.

After 1835 the slavery debate intensified. In the North, the Abolitionist movement became strident in its demand for the cessation of slavery. The South, on the other hand, grew irritated by what they saw as Northern hypocrisy and insensitivity. The same division began to polarize Baptists too. The condemnation or the defense of slavery, depending on regional perspective, became a frequent issue in the majority of churches.

Predictably, it broke into open discussion and controversy at the national level in the Triennial Conventions.

In 1840 a gathering called the "American Baptist Anti-Slavery Convention" was held in New York City. It was largely a product of radical antislavery sentiment among Baptists in the North. It also reflected the feelings and purpose of several missionaries in Burma who recently had severed their connection with the Triennial Convention. They had formed a new organization in order to work without association with slaveholders or those who supported them. Many Baptist leaders in the South perceived this meeting as a direct assault, and over the next several months a number of southern Baptist churches and organizations began to withhold funds and support from the Board of Foreign Missions and the American and Foreign Bible Society until they could be assured that those agencies were not influenced by abolitionism.

When the Triennial Convention met in 1841, open schism was barely avoided through consultations between caucuses, negotiated compromises, and declarations of neutrality. But such an attempt at a "middle way" was spurned by many on both sides of the issue, and for the next several years the issue festered in public and private correspondence, preaching, and associational activity. When the Triennial Convention met in 1844, it was in Philadelphia, and the North was more heavily represented than the South. Abolitionist supporters came prepared to actively promote their views. A resolution was passed that maintained a position of neutrality on the question of slavery but conceded the right of individuals to express their views on the subject.

Those in the North based their arguments on the principle of the dignity and worth of every individual and the moral wrong of slavery as a matter of divine principle. Southerners did not defend the evils of slavery, but they argued that it was an inherited disease that had to be cured slowly. On biblical grounds, they contended, Africans' contact with white masters enabled the former to hear and respond to the gospel. At the extremes, some abolitionist advocates demonized Southerners as being evil, while some Southern voices questioned the full humanity of Africans or claimed biblical precedent for suggesting that people of color were destined to be of secondary status.

Finally, at a meeting in 1845, the American Baptist Home Mission Society decided that it would be expedient for its members to carry on separate activities in the North and in the South. Almost immediately the Virginia Foreign Mission Society called for a convention. Meeting in Augusta, Georgia, over three hundred delegates from Southern churches met and determined to form the Southern Baptist Convention. Schism had occurred.

After the division, Baptists remaining from the Triennial Convention model of organization renamed their organization the "American Baptist Missionary Union" and continued its activity under the existing home and foreign mission societies and through the publication society. Later, these societies and many of the churches and associations supporting them would form an official convention.

notes
1. Minutes of the Philadelphia Baptist Association for 1820, 7–9. For more on the slavery debate, see Robert G. Torbet, *A History of the Baptists*, 3d ed. (Valley Forge, Pa.: Judson Press, 1963), 285.

chapter 8

new institutions for
a new century

In the twentieth century Baptists in the United States increasingly left the rural villages and small towns where their strength first had formed and, along with many others, flooded first into the cities and later into the suburbs of the growing urban nation. In 1850, it is estimated, there were some seven hundred thousand Baptists in a national population of about 22.5 million. By 1900 Baptists numbered about 4.2 million in a national population exceeding seventy-seven million. By century's end, Baptists would imprint their style, their values, and even their quarrels on much of the nation's consciousness. And Baptists in all their varieties would claim over 10 percent of the population of the United States.[1]

Between 1850 and 1900 the number of Baptist collegiate institutions grew from twenty-one to sixty, and their seminaries increased from two to five. Those numbers, too, would multiply in the century to come. While the discord that erupted in 1845 when Southerners left the Triennial Convention had not disappeared, by 1900 there was, nevertheless, a remarkable degree of cooperation among Baptists everywhere.

new organizations

The twentieth century had hardly begun when two Baptist organizations were born: the Baptist World Alliance and the Northern Baptist Convention (subsequently reorganized and renamed the American Baptist Convention, and then again later, the American Baptist Churches in the USA).

When the Northern Baptist Convention was formed in 1907, it was the result of over ten years of consideration about how the various mission societies might avoid duplication both of financial appeals and of administration and accounting concerns. The formation of the Convention was but the beginning of a lengthy and still incomplete process of searching for ways to effectively merge and magnify the work of the mission organizations.

The Northern Baptist Convention was organized out of the previous American Baptist Board of Education and Publication, along with the Foreign and Home Mission Boards that came out of the older American Baptist Missionary Union. Reflecting the age's optimistic spirit of unity and progress, this creation of a national denomination was perceived as a unifying of Baptist forces outside the South and the shaping of a more effective vision for mission rather than as a further definition of division between regions. When Freewill Baptists soon joined forces with the new Northern Baptist Convention in 1911, there was a lively hope that others, particularly Baptist organizations reflecting ethnic or cultural heritages, would follow.

As things turned out, however, the twentieth century did not fulfill the hopes of those who saw Baptist participation with other Christians as the ideal to be fulfilled, nor did it witness the development of genuine Baptist unity. In fact, it can be argued that by that century's end, Baptists were more fragmented, or at least more separately defined, than at its beginning. By the year 2000, many Baptists were skeptical of ecumenical movements or of interchurch cooperation beyond the most practical sharing of resources in mission or local community activities.

The American Baptists, always at the table for initial discussions of ecumenical endeavors such as the formation of the Federal, later the National, Council of Churches, often struggled with resistance from some within their constituency.[2] Southern Baptists, though greatly successful in developing a global, well-funded mission program, most often remained separate from ecumenical approaches to missions and concluded the century having endured several intense internal biblical and theological conflicts.

Still, the twentieth century was a "Baptist century," because Baptist churches continued a pattern of growth, Baptist missions had a profound influence on cultural and political change, and Baptist patterns of organization, process, and procedure became, whether intentionally or not, a way of American religious life and influenced its political and cultural institutional expression as well.

Transcending the geographical and cultural boundaries of Baptists in North America alone, the creation of the Baptist World Alliance in 1905 was a clear expression of the Baptist hunger for unity, particularly unity in forming a common global Baptist fellowship and vision. At its origin, a primary bond was defined in the connection between Baptists in Great Britain and North America. The desire to strengthen the bonds of fellowship between and among churches around the world, many of which had arisen from mission activity, was also strong. Recognizing the British roots of the Baptist movement, the first congress of the Alliance was held in London, and the presiding officer was the famous Scottish Baptist preacher Alexander Maclaren, then 79 years old. The first congress was a warm-spirited and markedly evangelical celebration attended by over three thousand people, 750 of whom came from beyond Britain.

At the beginning, the Alliance corporately expressed an optimism that the Baptists' basic evangelical and nonsacramental understanding of faith would prevail throughout the world. On the other hand, it also articulated a recognition that Baptists were but one family among many in "Christendom" and sought as one of their goals to work in a cooperative spirit with Christians everywhere. It was a delicate balance for Baptists, who often find it difficult to maintain a steady course of commitment to cherished principles while at the same time working effectively and cooperatively with each other and with other Christians.

Between congresses, the Alliance developed a style of functioning as a kind of "Baptist communications center" through a variety of commissions and committees enabling discussions on theological, ethical, historical, educational, worship, and other matters of interest to Baptists in their churches and in relationship to the cultures in which they lived. During times when factions within the Baptist world have been at odds, the Alliance has frequently been one of the few places where theological and institutional adversaries maintained fellowship and connection.

conflicting theologies

From its earliest days, the twentieth century clearly was to be one in which science and technology would change life in dramatic ways. In some ways, Baptists saw the opportunities for mission and growth contained in technology and industry and quickly adapted them to their purposes. Colporters began to drive cars and trucks rather than buggies and carts as they delivered religious tracts, Bibles, and Sunday school materials. American Baptists increased the number of railroad chapel cars dedicated to founding new churches as the railroads made possible missions and evangelization in even the remotest parts of the country. Baptist publication societies became even more productive as literacy increased and as more efficient transportation delivered materials into the hands of readers. In New York, the American Tract Society, strongly supported by many Baptists as well as by other evangelically minded Christians, became housed in one of the grand new skyscrapers that soon would define the city's skyline. In foreign missions, new and more reliable transportation and communication allowed missionaries to be sent more predictably and safely into new areas of outreach and enabled them to be in more frequent contact with their supporting agencies. There was reason to be optimistic that by means of modern systems, it would become a "Christian century"—a phrase by which one visionary Christian ecumenical magazine boldly named itself.

But for Baptists, there was also a growing sense of unease as modernity came into conflict with beliefs and traditions in the past. This conflict took place in various arenas, including science, with the growing popularity of Darwin's theory of evolution, and theology. The struggle between the "modernists" and the "fundamentalists" early in the century included factions within many Christian denominations. Baptists, however, were prominent on both sides of this divide and were especially affected by the conflict. From 1925 to 1945, New York City Baptist preacher Harry Emerson Fosdick was the most visible popular spokesperson for the modernist understanding of Scripture and its impact on the modern world.

The modernists, or as they were more frequently called, "liberals," came to see that the main task of the church was to reform society and to bring the kingdom of God to earth. They attempted to mediate between what they saw as a sometimes crude and uncritical evangelicalism and the new "scientific modernism." They were not, as they were sometimes accused, without faith or belief, being most often instead persons of great personal faith and devotion. But they understood that the modern age brought new insights and new obligations for interpreting the Bible, the traditions, and the priorities of the church.

Fundamentalists, in contrast, believed that the basis of religion itself was under attack by new and modern forces and therefore believed that any change or mediation in traditional approaches to biblical understanding or faith would encourage its demise. Baptists and others of this perspective received their name from a series of volumes that several Baptists (and others) published from 1910 to 1915 under the title *The Fundamentals*. As their name implied, they sought to reestablish personal atonement and salvation as the primary purpose of faith, and to do so they emphasized the inerrancy of Scripture and the deity of Jesus Christ, his virgin birth, the substitutionary nature of his death, his bodily resurrection, and his imminent and personal return to establish his kingdom on earth.[3] The revivalist Billy Sunday in the 1920s and, later in the post–World War II years, the evangelist Billy Graham and the intellectual Carl Henry were the most visible and famous of those who ably articulated the conservative position of fundamentalism.

Because most Baptists had only recently been exposed to the intellectual debates that undergirded the liberal position, most Baptists were, emotionally at least, sympathetic to the fundamentalist position. However, most Baptists also reacted negatively to an early fundamentalist proposal to safeguard orthodox doctrines in a creedal statement. Thus, fundamentalists generally failed to capture Baptist institutions even while they prevailed in capturing the spiritual allegiance of a great many Baptists. As a result, virtually every Baptist institution developed a continuing tension in faith and theology because of the strongly entrenched positions held by the liberal and the fundamentalist camps. The majority of people adhered to a broadly conservative middle ground, deeply committed to Baptist principles but often sympathetic to very conservative expressions of biblical interpretation and faith.

As the century progressed, this tension absorbed a great deal of energy and created much duplication of effort. Battles for control of mission boards and other organizations between fundamentalist and liberal groups continued for much of the century. The conflict was especially pronounced in the arena of theological and collegiate education. In the minds of many Baptists, the divinity school at the University of Chicago had been established in 1890 as a bulwark for faith against the rising tide of rationalism. But by the early twentieth century, its faculty included several representatives of theological liberalism. A similar tension developed in a number of Baptist or Baptist-related institutions.

Concerns about theological liberalism contributed to the establishment of more conservative institutions for training ministers and to a more evangelical approach to mission and ministry. Among them were two seminaries: Northern Baptist Theological Seminary, founded in 1913, and Eastern Baptist Theological Seminary, founded in 1925.

The work of education and mission societies was severely affected by the theological conflict. Debates regarding whether the policies of appointment of missionaries should be "inclusive" or "evangelical" occupied much of society time. Conservatives charged that missionaries who denied the virgin birth or other fundamentalist principles of belief were being appointed without caution. Liberals, on the other hand, resisted any creedal or formulary standard by reasserting the sufficiency of personal faith and acceptance of the Bible, especially the New Testament, as the guide to faith.

In the North, churches of extreme conservative views had drifted away from the Northern Baptist Convention during the 1920s and 1930s. Many of them affiliated with Southern Baptists or with one of several small conservative groups. Tensions within the Northern Baptist Convention came to a head when, in 1947 at a preconvention meeting, the Conservative Baptist Fellowship (formerly the Fundamental Fellowship) of the Convention organized as the Conservative Baptist Association of America. Despite a technical provision allowing churches to participate with the Conservative Baptist Association without withdrawing from other affiliations, for all practical purposes a new denomination of Baptists had been formed. This was cemented in 1948 when the group organized the Conservative

Baptist Home Mission Society, located in Chicago.

Southern Baptists, more homogeneous due to shared cultural and regional values and a robust conservative theology, managed their theological tensions without rupture. Still, there were conflicts in the South, especially in educational institutions, as churches often became identified with one camp or the other. Denominational division, however, would be delayed until the 1980s, when the institutional structure of the Southern Baptist Convention came under the control of ultraconservative leaders, causing more moderate and liberal churches to find new expression in organizations such as the Cooperative Baptist Fellowship and the Southern Baptist Alliance (later renamed the Alliance of Baptists), or in strong regional associations such as that in Texas, where the state convention, due to its size, essentially assumed denominational status on its own.

By the middle of the twentieth century, therefore, Baptists were divided by differences in theological and, often, political belief. Conservatives (the most extreme of which were labeled fundamentalists) adhered to a standard of literal biblical interpretation that was uncompromising in its adherence to the presumed truth of biblical authorship in general and specific texts in particular. By political orientation they tended toward conservatism, distrusted change, and, by emphasizing God's particular plan for America, were strongly patriotic.

In contrast, moderates (also known as liberals) allowed some latitude in interpreting the meaning of scriptural truth. In theology, as in biblical interpretation, they tolerated wider parameters of perspective. In political orientation liberals encouraged a global understanding of the affairs of nations and increasingly advocated the necessity of faith having an impact on issues of justice, human rights, and the cause of peace. In theology and preaching they emphasized a prophetic role of challenging the powers of civil and corporate establishment.

politics and society

These currents converged into the rough waters of the 1960s with particular vigor. For example, in the presidential election of 1960, conservative and fundamentalist Baptists reacted negatively to the nomination and subsequent election of John F. Kennedy because of his Roman Catholic identity, fearing that a Roman Catholic in the White House could not avoid following the dictates of the pope. Some in their opposition cited the Baptist principle of the separation of church and state. Liberals, on the other hand, tended to interpret the principle of separation of church and state as an argument that anyone might serve in the highest office as long as the candidate, as president, made allegiance to the United States Constitution and the American public a matter of higher precedence than obedience to a particular church in political matters.

Issues that divided the society in general during the 1960s and early 1970s also divided Baptists in both the North and the South. These issues included the Vietnam War and the civil rights and peace and freedom movements. Conservative Baptists emphasized traditional values, tended to support the status quo in both local and national policies, and favored a more gradual approach to the integration of churches, often siding with "separate but equal" philosophies of educational opportunity. Liberal Baptists were more likely to call for fundamental changes in the society and in the church. They emphasized the need for prophetic leadership, and in some cases they could be found in the front lines of demonstrations and acts of civil disobedience.

Although the most visible leader of the civil rights movement, Martin Luther King Jr., was a Baptist, even among African American Baptists support of open confrontation of unjust laws and practices was mixed, often along conservative versus liberal lines.[4] In fact, these divisions led to the establishment of the Progressive National Baptist Convention, which broke away from the National Baptist Convention in 1961.[5]

While virtually no practicing Baptists supported all the outcomes of the "sexual revolution," conservatives were much more likely than liberals to perceive this social revolution as the most important indicator of a catastrophic decline in morality. Liberals, on the other hand, were more likely to focus on identifying and addressing sin in the structures of society. Not surprisingly, conservatives and fundamentalists generally supported the Vietnam War, while liberals opposed it. Liberals also were more supportive of a new understanding of the roles of women in the church and in the society.

Baptists in the 1970s were motivated generally by concerns about declining standards of morality. They were especially alarmed by statistics indicating a rise in urban crime rates, drug use, and the high number of abortions following the Supreme Court decision *Roe v. Wade.* At the same time, the numerical and spiritual vitality of church life seemed to be diminishing in many churches. In response, moderate and liberal Baptists generally advocated a community and corporate approach, believing that growing social chaos was largely the result of political and social inequities. Conservatives, in contrast, placed their emphasis on individual responsibility. Their approach tended to support religious conversion and renewal and programs of spiritual and moral "character building."

television

In this climate of moral reform, a number of religious personalities, many of them Baptist, explored and perfected far more effective ways to make use of modern media, especially television. Some "televangelists" came to consider the broadcast audience, rather than a studio audience or a church congregation, to be their true "congregation" and spoke directly to them. This technique placed a high premium on interactive dialogue, dramatic skill, dynamic interaction with the camera, and the creation of effective channels for the broadcast audience to respond or feel as if they were responding.[6]

The most successful among the television broadcasters carefully avoided theological controversy, instead casting their messages in clear, simple terms and claiming to root their messages in tradition. Because modern biblical interpretation increasingly relies on knowledge of a wide, complex body of information regarding history, archaeology, textual analysis, and other disciplines, the message of television educators and evangelists exerted a strong appeal in its simple, more easily understood approach.[7] In subtle ways, it successfully created the impression that those who made biblical understanding "complicated" probably were guilty of corrupting its timeless message. Such "liberals," therefore, increasingly were portrayed as corrupters of the gospel message and also were cast as "intellectuals"—a description that Baptists had always found troublesome, as the Baptist movement had never been strongest among educated groups and because of the elitism that "intellectualism" implied.

Finally, radio and television preachers nearly always connected their message to a sense of urgency that required response from their audience. The requested response ranged from prayer or prayer requests to political action and public support of programs that they offered. These programs always promised to rectify moral wrongs or defend against those who might harm the faith and values of the audience. And, of course, embedded in the urgency of their message was an appeal for financial support.

In establishing this technique, these televangelists and their colleagues recognized the need for continued, sustained, personal communication, and they adopted first an ability to record and track communications from those who responded with either donations or requests, and later developed highly sophisticated techniques for mass mailings both to ignite interest and to gain financial contributions. They generally were highly effective in identifying persons receptive to their message who would generously support their agenda. Indeed, they were so effective that their example became a model for a similar approach to defining political constituencies that ultimately transformed American political organization and identification in the last quarter of the twentieth century.

An early pioneer in the use of the media was Billy Graham, who mastered the use of radio and television for his evangelistic crusades. These were, however, essentially passive events for the broadcast audience, punctuated with personal messages or testimonies in place of traditional television advertisements. The technique was refined and developed by many others, including the faith healer Katherine Kuhlman, "power of positive thinking" disciple Robert Schuller, and others.

No one, however, understood the potential for both political and religious persuasion better than two independent, self-styled Baptist television personalities, Pat Robertson and Jerry Falwell. As a result of their success, they were consulted by national political leaders and became frequent guests at the White House (Robertson himself launched an exploratory candidacy for president in 1988).

The public success of Falwell and Robertson, especially, had profound consequences for Baptists. Neither Falwell nor Robertson were "mainstream" Baptists, and neither had more than a casual connection to an organized Baptist denominational structure, although Falwell later identified himself as a Southern Baptist in the 1990s. But their high visibility and success in the public eye created the illusion that they were Baptist spokespersons, and their conservative theology and political agendas came to be equated with an official Baptist position in the perception of a great many people, including Baptist church members. As a result, Baptists were perceived increasingly in the public mind to be universally fundamentalist in theology and conservative in political orientation. Baptists who represented moderate or liberal theological, biblical, or political positions found themselves increasingly misunderstood. Some of them abandoned their Baptist association.

In short, Baptists were viewed as a significant part of the creation of the late-twentieth-century American political and social phenomenon popularly known as the "Religious Right," and were perceived to be a more universal part of its agenda than they really were.

notes

1. These figures are derived from Robert G. Torbet, *A History of the Baptists*, 3d ed. (Valley Forge, Pa.: Judson Press, 1963), 424, and from an approximation of the totals for the largest Baptist bodies as listed in the *Yearbook of American and Canadian Churches* (Nashville: Abingdon, 2000). The accuracy of church membership lists is notoriously difficult to assess, as is that of United States census figures.

2. Northern Baptists (since 1950, American Baptists) were part of the Federal Council of Churches from 1908 and continued after its reorganization as the National Council of Churches in 1950. They also were participants in the beginning of the World Council of Churches in 1948. At times they have faced severe opposition to such participation from within their churches, primarily because some believed that the National or World Councils were led by theological liberals or, especially during the Cold War era, by communists. Southern Baptists never have been full members of the Federal or National Councils, or later the World Council, primarily because of the same concerns expressed by opponents with the American Baptist churches, but also due to apprehensions that membership might threaten the independence of the local church, concerns regarding some of the Council's social justice programs, and reservations about the National Council's tradition of pacifism in response to war. Perhaps their strongest objection, however, is that interdenominational cooperation jeopardizes two important Baptist principles: religious liberty, especially the separation of church and state; and the necessity of personal decisions for salvation. Simply by being officially associated with churches that do not share these principles, they believe, their own commitments and principles would be compromised. Southern Baptists have, however, frequently availed themselves of programs of the National Council, especially Bible translations and materials prepared for Christian education. They also, on some occasions, have been official observers at Council proceedings.

3. "Substitutionary atonement" is the doctrine that Jesus Christ, in his death, substituted himself as the required sacrifice to God that made all other sacrifices unnecessary, including that of the individual seeking to be saved.

4. Among African American Baptists the issue certainly was not one of defending racial injustice or of articulating a biblical view that supported racial superiority. Rather, it was a social and political conservatism that reflected, in part, a concern that overt political activity might threaten the black community and its institutions that caused some leaders, including Baptist ministers, to be skeptical of prophetic and political challenges to the status quo.

5. The Progressive Baptist Convention of America was formed by former leaders and participants in the National Baptist Convention USA who objected to what they saw as its "autocratic rule." They were advocates and supporters of Martin Luther King Jr., and they favored more forthright approaches to addressing racism in American life. Prominent leaders in establishing the new convention included Gardner C. Taylor, Martin Luther King Sr., Martin Luther King Jr., Ralph David Abernathy, and Benjamin Mays, all of whom already had achieved or later would achieve national recognition for their efforts in improving education, promoting civil rights, redressing poverty, and providing pastoral leadership.

6. An early master of this technique was Robert Schuller, who, though not a Baptist, attracted a broad following among Baptists for his *Hour of Power* television broadcast and heavily influenced Baptist leaders who sought to emulate both his strategy and his success. Schuler's "Crystal Cathedral" is artfully constructed to suggest a classic worship center in modern architectural style, but effectively serves as a television sound stage for an audience far beyond its specific location. Many Baptists who chose his approach ultimately left behind any semblance of traditional church architecture and reshaped worship around a stage and set style of presentation, even if television broadcasting was not a routine part of their weekly programming.

7. One exception, however, was the approach of some television preachers who established themselves as "experts" in matters having to do with ancient mysteries, numerology, and the end of history especially, and who, therefore, were revered as guides to understanding matters beyond the comprehension of ordinary people.

chapter 9

moving to the center
of american life

Perhaps the most important Baptist story of the twentieth century is not that of the divisions and controversy, but that of the movement of Baptists to the center of American social and political life. In the late nineteenth and twentieth centuries Baptists were more frequently represented in state and national legislatures, but few achieved national positions of visibility or influence. Notable exceptions included prominent, wealthy leaders such as James B. Colgate and John D. Rockefeller. Both had risen from humble origins and retained the religious loyalties of their childhood.

But by the end of the twentieth century, Baptists epitomized the great center of social, educational, political, and religious life in the United States. One symbol of this shift was the rise to prominence of a number of Baptist leaders on a national scale. These leaders took Baptist principles of freedom, equality, and passion for change—even if their visions for change differed—and applied them to concerns of the national and international arenas. They exercised influence far beyond Baptist circles.

rising political prominence

Charles Evans Hughes was the first Baptist of the twentieth century to achieve national political prominence. A lifelong Baptist who attended Colgate University (then Madison University) and Brown University, both Baptist institutions, Hughes later served as the first president of the Northern Baptist Convention (later the ABCUSA). He served as governor of New York from 1906 until 1910, and in that same year he was appointed as an associate justice of the United States Supreme Court. Following the split in the Republican party between rivals William Howard Taft and Theodore Roosevelt, who took his loyalists out to form the "Bull Moose" party, the Republicans drafted Hughes as their presidential candidate in 1916. In that election, he lost to Woodrow Wilson by the narrow margin of 277 to 254 amidst speculation that, had the Republicans remained united, he would have won. He later served both Presidents Harding and Coolidge as secretary of state. He resisted continuing invitations to run for the presidency, including an urgent request that he run against Franklin D. Roosevelt in 1932, which he rejected on the grounds that he was, at the age of seventy, "too old." Hughes was widely admired for his fairness and his skill as a mediator, and often enjoyed bipartisan confidence and support. He was appointed chief justice of the Supreme Court by President Hoover in 1930, and served admirably and honorably as one of the most influential chief justices of the century until his retirement in 1941.

Harold E. Stassen, a Baptist layperson, was elected as the "boy wonder" reform governor of Minnesota from 1938 to 1943, when he resigned to join the navy. Following World War II,

having achieved success and significant national attention, especially as a representative to the commission that created the
United Nations and as a leader in drafting its charter in 1947,
he competed for the Republican nomination for president in
1948, losing to New York governor Thomas E. Dewey. He
served as president of the University of Pennsylvania, and then
sought the nomination for the United States presidency again
in 1952, losing this time to Dwight D. Eisenhower. He became
Eisenhower's trusted friend, and he served in his administration
for five years. Later, Stassen was appointed to a number of
national and international positions of counsel and cooperation. Unlike Hughes, to an advanced age he continued to offer
himself as a candidate for the presidency, partly to assure continued national discussion of issues of international peace, dis-
armament, and justice. Stassen was an active Northern (later
American) Baptist and served his denomination as its president.

Harry S. Truman, a Southern Baptist from Missouri, was
chosen out of relative obscurity to serve as Franklin D. Roosevelt's second vice president. In 1945 he became president
upon Roosevelt's death, and in 1948 he won his own presidential term in a hotly contested election against Republican
Thomas E. Dewey. Truman at first was ridiculed for his inexpe-
rience and modest credentials. However, in the view of many,
he became the strongest president of the twentieth century,
guiding the nation through the difficult months concluding
World War II, the postwar years, and the beginning of the Cold
War. Throughout his terms he earned the popular title "Give
'Em Hell Harry" for his renowned plain speaking and blunt
expression. In and out of office, Truman's down-to-earth

personality, expressed in a pungent style of independent thinking, seemed to symbolize a Baptist style. While in office, Truman frequently attended Baptist worship services, often walking
to church on Sunday mornings, and on occasion he consented
to address young people on the importance of Sunday school
and church participation.

the civil rights movement

Perhaps the most significant rise to leadership in the middle of
the twentieth century came from the ranks of African American
churches. As a matter of survival, many African American
churches had retained an inward, self-protective stance regarding their environment. But the migration of many African
American men and women from poor, rural areas into the cities,
where employment might be available, ultimately gave rise to a
variety of strong African American congregations in urban
areas, a great many of them Baptist.

In New York City in the 1920s, Adam Clayton Powell Sr.
opened one of the first "soup kitchens" soon after his church, the
Abyssinian Baptist Church, moved into Harlem. His son, Adam
Clayton Powell Jr., expanded the church's outreach to include
welfare work and employment placement and offered support to
black workers in strikes and attempts to unionize.[1] Powell himself became an active strategist in confronting economic issues
and the emerging problems of civil rights. He was elected to the
New York city council, and in 1944 he became the first black
congressional representative from New York State, indeed from
the East, and during his lengthy service in Washington he
emerged as a powerful leader in Congress, eventually chairing

the House Committee on Education and Labor.[2]

Leon Sullivan, pastor of Philadelphia's Zion Baptist Church, who had served under the tutelage of Powell Sr. in Harlem, was another African American Baptist leader who left a powerful mark on twentieth-century political life. Beginning with a "selective patronage campaign" in the late 1950s, Sullivan implemented a successful boycott of a number of consumer-oriented corporations, with black employment as a goal. As the strategy proved successful, he developed a variety of methods to help provide technical training and skill development for black workers. These programs emerged in 1964 in the Opportunities Industrialization Centers of America, which networked programs for training, skill development, and job placement. Sullivan later became the first black person to sit on the board of General Motors, and he expanded his interests and energies into the problems of black workers in South Africa under apartheid. His "Sullivan Principles" were adopted by some American companies.[3] Sullivan, like Powell Sr., established a pathway by which African American Baptists took the gospel from the pulpit into the marketplace and the political arena as a means of outreach, mission, and activism.

Undoubtedly, however, Martin Luther King Jr. became the most visible Baptist of the century. King's biography is so well known that it suffices here to recall that he was the son of a gifted Baptist minister, trained for the ministry, and functioned as both a traditional minister in a parish context and as a "prophet to the nations" on a global scale, and that his legacy transcends specific issues or agendas. That King was the center-piece of the civil rights movement is without debate. But even more important, King's command of the biblical pulpit oratory of Southern preachers and the "social gospel" insights of Northern theologians, his natural gifts of charisma and leadership, and his broad vision that the oppressed, disadvantaged condition of American black people was, in important ways, connected to the experience of all people, made his leadership between 1955 and 1968 a profound moment of transformation that was historically American, profoundly biblical, and uniquely Baptist.

The civil rights movement in the United States was largely led by black clergy or by sons (and a few daughters) of clergy, and through the framework of the black church "provided an ideological framework through which passive attitudes were transformed into a collective consciousness supportive of collective action."4 The clarity of the consciousness was articulated in Martin Luther King's oratory, and the nature of the collective action was tempered by his vision. Without Martin Luther King, the battle for opportunity and equality for blacks in American public and private life might have succumbed to overt violence in confrontation with white establishment traditions or might have drifted into racial, social, and economic separatism and a de facto apartheid that inevitably would have prolonged the lack of workable relations between white and black Americans. Such a result also would have confused the outcomes of the growing diversity in America that eventually reflected not only immigrants of European and African origins, but also those from Latin America, Asia, and virtually everywhere else on the globe.

Through the power of his personal charisma and gifts, and also through the work of his organization, the Southern

Christian Leadership Conference, King's leadership also assured that the civil rights movement would be influenced by the language and values of the church, especially Baptist rhetoric and style. King's untimely death in 1968 sealed forever his emblematic leadership of the peace and freedom movement and gave the United States a martyr who in death may have exceeded even his achievements in life as a symbol of justice and reconciliation.

King's Baptist legacy and political vision were carried forward by a group of young leaders who, after his death, rose to prominence in continuing leadership that quickly spread to traditional, mainstream expressions. For example, Andrew Young served as mayor of one of the deep South's major cities, Atlanta, and later in the United Nations; William Gray continued in a pastoral role in Philadelphia while also serving in the House of Representatives, where ultimately he rose to its third most powerful position as majority whip; Walter Fauntroy persisted as pastor of a church in Washington, D.C., while also serving as a leader, representative, and spokesperson in local and national capacities. Jesse Jackson, an early claimant to King's leadership mantle, marshaled his considerable oratorical gifts and political skills into a reform-oriented political organization, the Rainbow Coalition, later mounted two credible campaigns for president, and achieved a role as "statesman-at-large" in national and world affairs. The fact that all of these men were ordained Baptist clergy and that others, especially several female leaders such as Congressional luminaries Barbara Jordan and Shirley Chisolm, had clear connections to Baptist traditions through involvement in churches or having been born to ministers made the Baptist imprint on the vision for a new America very strong.

the white house

In addition to the clear African American Baptist presence in the mid-century social restructuring and reform, Jimmy Carter's election as president of the United States in the bicentennial year of 1976 further affirmed the mainstream, rising tide of Baptists. Carter's genuine faith, forthright manner, and strong moral consciousness made him an appealing candidate to the American public in the first election following the Watergate scandal and the painful national experience of President Nixon's resignation in disgrace. Carter was a "small-town boy" who had grown up a Baptist and credited Baptist church life with some of his early goals and the formation of his personal integrity. Furthermore, he credited his boyhood knowledge of the work of missionaries with opening his interest in foreign affairs. In particular reference to the then looming challenge of establishing diplomatic relations with China, he confessed that he always had thought the missionaries working in China to be a kind of "elite group."[5]

During Carter's presidency the importance of his church connections remained clearly visible. When his home church in Georgia proved to be inhospitable to persons of color, Carter and others withdrew to form a new church based on racial openness and theological moderation. Carter actively supported that congregation while in office, and when he returned to his home in Plains, Georgia, he resumed a key role in its leadership and teaching. In Washington, D.C., Carter and his family attended the First Baptist Church, and they, as a family, officially joined the congregation soon after their arrival in the White House.

Even more than his church participation, however, Carter's highly moral approach to both domestic and international affairs clearly revealed the degree to which his faith values determined his approach to national and international leadership. In his performance as a former president, Carter developed a career that is without parallel among his peers. His several books minimized any defense of his policies, a practice which usually preoccupies retired presidents, and instead dealt squarely with ongoing issues that demanded American national attention. His later writing especially focused on matters of faith and the human spirit. His devotion to the causes of world peace, punctuated by several significant rounds of international negotiation, all of which required high levels of trust and sensitivity, marked him as a world leader who set the standards for others. His devotion to human need, notably his support of Habitat for Humanity, demonstrated his continued concern for the poor. In Jimmy Carter the nation and the world witnessed an important Baptist illustration of spiritual vocation at work.

For the last eight years of the century, the American president again came from Baptist roots. Bill Clinton came to office having been a faithful church member in a Little Rock, Arkansas, Southern Baptist church while serving as governor, and crediting a recently deceased Southern Baptist pastor as having been a most important inspiration, mentor, and ethical guide. His first inauguration was held the morning after twelve hundred Baptists greeted him in prayer and celebration at Washington D.C.'s First Baptist Church. That service and the official inaugural ceremonies both featured Baptist leaders and preachers, including journalist and creative media personality Bill Moyers and prominent Brooklyn pastor Gardner C. Taylor.

Clinton remained a popular president throughout his eight years in office despite his personal failings. History will pass its own judgment on his presidency and his personal conduct. One might say that in Bill Clinton, Baptists themselves experienced a "coming of age" socially, politically, and culturally.[6] Rising from ordinary circumstances, he became a Rhodes scholar and a master, some say genius, of political process and conflict. In many respects he guided the nation through one of its most successful decades. Yet his flaws were equally evident. In a sense, Clinton as president was a Baptist "Everyman"—gifted and successful in ways anyone could envy, but flawed and capable of self-destruction in ways anyone could fear.

the "baptist century"

In sum, by the end of the twentieth century, the extraordinary diversity of belief and expression among Baptists had become clear at the highest levels of public office. During the Clinton administration, for example, someone noted that in the event of national disaster the constitutionally defined presidential succession would have to descend through five levels before someone other than a Baptist would accede to the office. Former Speaker of the House Newt Gingrich of Georgia, architect of the "Conservative Revolution" of the early 1990s, is a Baptist, as is former Alabama Representative John Buchanan, then the executive for the liberal advocacy organization People for the American Way. Jesse Helms, from North Carolina, a long-term powerful Republican Senate voice for conservative causes, is a Baptist, as is Mark Hatfield of Oregon, also a long-term but moderate Republican senator who often was regarded as one of the Senate's moral guides.[7] Some Baptists lobbied to "return prayer to the public schools," while others lobbied against it.

In the United States by the end of the twentieth century, it seemed that Baptists were present in every rank and station of American life and were strongly represented in the growing racial and cultural diversity of the nation.[8] Baptists had broadly influenced other organizations, religious and secular alike, with their participatory style of governance, their inclination to lay open their innermost concerns to public investigation, their undying confidence in "a better way and a better day," and their propensity for contentious, conflicted debate over many things that matter—and over a few that do not.

notes
1. C. Eric Lincoln and Lawrence H. Mamiya, *The Black Church in the African American Experience* (Durham, N.C.: Duke University Press, 1990), 121.
2. Ibid., 210–11.
3. Ibid., 263–64.
4. Aldon Morris, cited in Lincoln and Mamiya, *Black Church*, 165.
5. Jimmy Carter, *Keeping Faith: Memoirs of a President* (New York: Bantam Books, 1982), 186.
6. Bill Clinton came to the presidency with a clear heritage as a long-term Southern Baptist by affiliation and association. During his first year in office he alternated worship in Baptist church contexts and in Methodist churches (the denomination of Hillary Clinton's affiliation), and then later most regularly worshiped in the Methodist church. In the aftermath of "Monicagate" he received spiritual counsel from several ministers, both Methodist and Baptist.
7. Helms and Hatfield have retired from public office.
8. In the latter part of the twentieth century, Baptist growth was most rapid and extensive among minority racial groups, especially Asian and Latino populations.

section three

basic baptist beliefs

chapter 10

the bible and theology

Thus far, we have taken a historical approach to understanding where Baptists came from and how they developed. That story is, of course, unfinished, with new chapters now being written as Baptists around the world continue to define their identity and practice their faith. At this point, then, it will be helpful to focus on what Baptists have believed about the Bible, theology and faith, the church and its workings, and Baptists in relationship to the community and world around them. Of course, the individualism and independence of Baptists makes virtually any statement about Baptist beliefs subject to challenge. Nevertheless, we can describe what the main themes of Baptist faith have been in the past.

core beliefs and confession

Regardless of the times and circumstances in which Baptists have found themselves, some basic, fundamental beliefs have tended to shape and direct what Baptists have done, individually and together. Baptists have shared views about the nature of God, the nature and experience of humankind, the character and role of the church, and aspects of faith such as the nature of salvation, the beginning and the end of the world, and the nature of Jesus Christ.

From their earliest beginnings, Baptists have held Scripture (the Bible) to be the highest source of understanding and the most authoritative guide for belief. This is part of their heritage from the Reformation. Some early Baptist leaders also were scholars and were aware of early church traditions and beliefs. At times, these leaders chose to reconsider and restate expressions of earlier church traditions rather than simply to reject them.

Thus, from time to time, Baptists (especially early Baptists) have sought to summarize their beliefs in the form of a "confession" of faith. These include the London Confession (1644 and 1677), the Philadelphia Confession (1742), and the New Hampshire Confession (1833). Early Baptist expressions of faith also were shaped by the confessions of the Waterlander Mennonites (1580) and by the True Confession (1596) of the English Separatists in Amsterdam.

These documents were rarely used in the way that some church groups have used similar expressions: as a summary of appropriate belief, as a test of orthodoxy, or as a resource for worship wherein all are united in one voice of faith. Rather, they were expressions about general themes that defined relationships among church members, between members and churches, and among churches.

All Baptist confessions agree on the primary role of Scripture, the Trinitarian nature of God, and the unique, specific role of Jesus Christ as God's Son and the agent of salvation. Baptist confessions also demonstrate a clear connection to the historic early creeds of the universal Christian church, such as the

Nicene Creed (325), the Apostles' Creed (ca. 500), and others. Baptist beliefs are deeply rooted in ancient Christian experience.

In times of controversy, Baptist confessions have served as convenient guides to discern what Baptists have believed in the past in order to clarify what Baptists might believe in the present. Conversely, they have been used to measure whether a change in expression of belief might be considered. But an important first understanding about Baptist belief is that Baptists generally have not been a "confessional people." That is, individual independence and responsibility in matters of faith, and individual church independence in practicing disciplines of faith, have taken precedence over any one statement of faith or belief that might require conformity. Early in their experience, Baptists established themselves as "noncreedal" in their experience of faith.

god and humankind

However, Baptists have been in common agreement about the nature of God. That is, from earliest times until now, Baptists have declared that God is one being, expressed in three manifestations: Father, Son, and Holy Spirit. God is the "uncreated Creator" and the eternal "I am." God is revealed in the older texts of Scripture as the "God of Abraham, Isaac, and Jacob," but also is revealed in the newer texts of Scripture as the "God and Father of our Lord Jesus Christ," in whom the revelation is finally and completely made. Baptists have also believed that it is through the convicting and converting power of the Holy Spirit that God works among humankind, and they have believed that the Holy Spirit proceeds from the Father and the

Son to confront human beings with their sin and to offer them the hope and the reality of salvation.

Baptists generally have believed that sin characterizes the nature of humankind, and that the presence of sin is the reason for the need for God's redemptive activity. In general, Baptists believe that humankind was created in the image and likeness of God, but that early people chose to disobey God and thereby fell from a perfect state of sinlessness into a state of sin. Some Baptists have believed that the fall of Adam and Eve was merely an example of this sin, while others have asserted that the sin of Adam and Eve in the garden of Eden was itself the cause of the universal presence of sin. In any case, it is the presence of sin that has encouraged a general sense that every person must become aware of his or her own "conviction" for sin and thus the need for God's intervention to overcome it.

Even the most Calvinistic of early Baptists, the Particular Baptists, refused to believe that God had selected some for damnation while marking others for salvation. Instead, they were confident that those who continued to choose sin and destruction rather than life in Christ condemned themselves. The Particular Baptists, whose tradition became dominant, contributed the belief that only through the intervening grace of Christ did any person have the possibility of salvation. The Arminian-influenced General Baptists, however, had a stronger sense that in Christ, God provided a moral example, and that the way to overcome sin was in greater attention to moral righteousness and good works with Christ as the example and enabler. Both perspectives of faith have continued in Baptist traditions until the present.

Baptists ultimately reached nearly universal agreement on the role of sin in human nature among the very young. Those Baptists who believed that human sin was primarily evident in human beings' propensity to choose sin did not believe that children could properly be understood to be sinful until they had reached an age at which they are capable of making moral choices. Baptists who tended to believe that all human beings inherited their sinful natures as a result of the fall of Adam and Eve nevertheless did not believe that children were to be held responsible for their sin until they had reached an age of moral choice. This led Baptists to reject the idea that children were "guilty" of sin. Although this subject continued to be discussed and debated in early Baptist experience, ultimately all Baptists agreed that the baptism of children prior to an age of responsibility was at the least not required, and was in any case not effective. Thus, Baptists have reserved baptism for adults, or at least for those old enough to choose it.

jesus christ and salvation

Baptists in general have always been a Christocentric people. That is, Baptists believe that Christ is Lord, exemplar of life, and living evidence of God. Early Baptist writings focus heavily on the nature and roles of Christ. Early Baptist expressions, particularly in the several Baptist confessions, assert that Christ is the Son of God, born of the Virgin Mary, fully God and fully human, and therefore in the most specific sense, the incarnate deity. Their profound sense of the sinfulness of humankind led them to define Christ's most critical role as that of the reconciler between humanity and God. In his life and especially in his death, Christ revealed God's love and was the embodiment of God's infinite grace.

In short, Baptists universally have believed that in the person of Jesus Christ, as demonstrated in his life, as present in his teachings, and as exemplified in his death and resurrection, there was historically presented the fullest and most complete revelation of God. For Baptists, therefore, Christ is "prophet, priest, and king." Furthermore, he is the mediator of the new covenant, and in him is the fulfillment of the Law and the Prophets of the ancient Hebrew Scriptures. Baptists believe that God has spoken many words to human beings, and that in the personalities of the Bible, and even in the personalities of history, portions of God's word may be heard, but that only in Christ is God's complete and last Word known.

For Baptists, the individual result of salvation is a growing sense of the knowledge and grace of Christ within, and with that, a growing experience of faith, hope, inner peace, and love. There is also, however, a strong communal and relational dimension to salvation. Baptists have believed that the salvation that is possible only in Christ brings forgiveness of sin and transforms the believer into a new creation. It is here that the common Baptist use of the phrase "born again" has a specific meaning, for the believer is "born again" or "transformed" by the Holy Spirit as a response to faith in Christ.

Baptists assert that salvation is ultimately a transformational experience not only for the individual, but also for the individual's relationships. That is, the new Christian becomes a disciple of Christ and seeks to follow Christ in allowing God to reshape and order his or her relationships and purposes in life.

77

Baptists therefore have traditionally spoken of giving "witness" or "testimony" in the hope of having an effect on others. This witness is seen in the fellowship of the local church as a place of mutual support and encouragement in spirit, but it is not limited to the church and in fact can penetrate beyond individual or church relationships into an effective transformation of a whole society. The dynamics of the Baptist concept of salvation frequently have made Baptists a powerful force for social change far beyond their local communities and have shaped their organizational life with a strong impulse for outreach and mission.

scripture

For most Baptists, not all of Scripture is regarded with equal weight. From their earliest beginnings, Baptists have tended to view the Old Testament, or more properly, the ancient Hebrew texts, through the corrective lenses of the New Testament, or Christian Scriptures. It is very clear that for Baptists, the New Testament provided the prototype of the church and the guidelines for faithful living and appropriate worship. Therefore, the Baptist appeal to biblical authority has always been primarily an appeal to the authority of the New Testament.

In addition, Baptists generally have viewed all the texts of the Bible through the revelation of God in Christ. Baptists have a high and sacred view of Christ (highly exalting his divinity as well as recognizing his humanity), and their experience of Christ has tended to be very personal in encountering the transformational experience of salvation. Therefore, their perspective on the interpretation of Scripture through their understanding of Christ often has been highly individualistic. It also, throughout

Baptist history, has tended to be colored by the more general personal experiences of individual Baptists and groups of Baptists, so that the interpretation of texts and meanings has reflected context and circumstance more often than it has reflected traditions of scholarship.

For this reason, especially since the late nineteenth century, Baptist views of Scripture at times have been a source of profound disagreement and conflict among Baptists themselves. Beginning in the nineteenth century, some have sought to interpret the Bible in ways consistent with the growing influence of modern scientific, literary, historical, archaeological, and psychological knowledge. Others have insisted that the Bible's authority can be affirmed only through the most literal reading and interpretation.

eschatology

Like most Christians, Baptists have sought to make sense of human experience from the perspective of the beginnings and endings of things. Because Baptists have such a strong reliance upon Scripture, they generally have not been attracted to philosophical debates about the origin of the universe, the preexistence or emergence of Christ, or other baffling issues with which some theological traditions have engaged. The story of creation as found in Genesis, whether interpreted literally or metaphorically, has sufficed to assure most Baptists of the primacy of God in creation and in God's governance of the universe.

About eschatology, or "end times," however, Baptists have expressed wide diversity of thought and belief. Some early Baptist writings reflect a fascination with the end times. The First

London Confession speaks of the time when the "Kingdom shall be then fully perfected when he shall the second time come in glory to reigne among his Saints . . . when he shall put all rule and authority under his feet, that the glory of the Father may be full and perfectly manifested in his Sonne, and the glory of the Father and the Sonne in all his members."[1]

However, neither the London document nor later confessions or official expressions succumbed to the temptation to speculate on specific dates or circumstances. In fact, Baptists in England remained remarkably free from the fervent millennialism that was rampant in England from the mid-seventeenth to the early-nineteenth centuries. We may assume that this was due in part to the difficulty that Baptists had in finding agreement on any particulars.

Generally, with rare, notable exceptions such as William Miller in New York in the nineteenth century, Baptist preaching has avoided the specific determination of end times and events that has caused embarrassment and a loss of credibility for the church. Instead, eschatological (end-time) discourse most often has focused on more personal concerns about eternal judgment and its consequences rather than on coming times of judgment on earth.

Generally, when Baptists have spoken of heaven and hell, it has been to distinguish between God's kingdom and the realm of evil. Early Baptists were much more focused on the certainty of eternal salvation for the faithful than they were on the likelihood of damnation or destruction. Indeed, what is striking about early Baptist writing is their essential optimism about God's dealing with humankind, on condition of faith. Damnation as a consequence for those who rejected Christ and his offer of salvation is more often an implied understanding than a described reality. One explanation for this ambiguity may be that early Baptists lived under conditions in which threats of one sort or another had been used to coerce their faithfulness or obedience to a creed or code. Thus, understandably they were averse to the use of dire threats in theological language of their own.

It also is true that Baptists have consistently had a "this worldly" view of the benefits of belief, focusing on moral behavior, vitality in the church, and strong expressions of the power of faith for life rather than on the terrors of faithlessness or on the rewards of an afterlife. This was a point of unity for later Baptists who emphasized social consciousness and those who emphasized personal righteousness as articulated in the evangelical piety that developed in the nineteenth century.

Baptists individually may believe in heaven or hell, and may from time to time have conceptions of Christ's return in millennial circumstances. Broadly and generally, however, Baptist people have been much more focused on the evidence of faith in life as it is lived in the present. And the place where most Baptists focus their lives in faith is the church.

notes
1. The First London Confession, Article XX, in William L. Lumpkin, ed., *Baptist Confessions of Faith* (Philadelphia: Judson Press, 1959), 162.

chapter 11

the church

Baptists believe in the "universal church," but they root their experience in the "local church." In this distinction Baptists depart from many Christians who place their commitment first in at least an expression of the universal church, and who understand the local church as only one small part of the greater whole.

We recall that the very earliest Baptists held the view that the church was universal, but they recognized that a particular expression of the church might be in error or corrupt. With such a view, one major challenge erupted in the question of how to determine what the right expression of the church ought to be, and how to determine when a church had become so flawed that it was no longer effective as a church. Much of the Reformation and its aftermath in Europe and elsewhere were devoted to debate, sometimes to the point of conflict, over that general concern.

Early on, Baptists addressed this problem. First, they concluded that the only valid prescriptions for the church were found in the New Testament. Further, they determined that while the universal church was real and vital, it was invisible and

known only to God. While affirming the reality and importance of the universal church, they placed their emphasis on the
local church—that small, intimate fellowship of people who
were known to each other, who made and observed commitments both to living life in faith and in commitment to their
fellowship, and who had experienced "believer's baptism" as a
rite and ritual of acceptance into the church.

By shaping this simple perspective, Baptists set themselves
free from attempts to determine whether others had the "right
theology" or the "right belief," and also cleared themselves from
any obligation to determine whether other churches or other
fellowships of Christians were correct in all their practices of
worship, organization, and activity. They had their opinions, of
course, and frequently expressed them, but they had neither
obligation nor expectation that they would impede others in
their beliefs. As a result, Baptists developed a lofty view of the
local congregation as the highest expression of life in faith.

For Baptists, Christ is the one and true foundation of the
church—not only the universal church, but also, specifically, the
local church. In that local church, Christ is "prophet, priest, and
king." As early Baptist John Smyth expressed it, "Christ only is
the king and lawgiver of the church and conscience."[1] Christ is
king and lawgiver of the whole church, to be sure, but for each
congregation of Baptists, that meant that Christ was head of
their particular church. And that was where they focused.

In sum, the church is, for Baptists, a fellowship gathering of
like-minded, saved individuals. In that fellowship the word of
God is proclaimed, heard, and interpreted. The purpose of the
fellowship of the church is in part to support and enable the

word of God to be shared beyond the church in the world, both in missions and in the personal witness of the church's individual members. And the church is to provide support for the members themselves as a place where faith is maintained and where the challenges of life issues and concerns may be faced, endured, and overcome.

worship

The church also is a worshiping fellowship. Baptists worship in many styles and forms, from the least formal to the most structured, and from strictly liturgical to freely charismatic. But all Baptist worship has two powerful motivations. The first is to give glory to the presence of God and thanksgiving for the saving presence of Christ. The second is to inspire and to strengthen individual members in their spiritual journey and Christian witness. Unlike some Christian denominations, Baptists generally do not view worship as an end in itself, but as a means to greater effectiveness in mission or as a launching point for a heightened personal effectiveness in providing a "witness" or example of Christ-like behavior in the world.

Baptists generally do not have a highly developed sense of formal ritual in worship. This is due in part to the Baptist conviction that there are only two ordinances that Jesus requires of the church and its worship: baptism and the Lord's Supper. Some contemporary Baptists use the terms "ordinance" and "sacrament" interchangeably, because "sacrament" implies a deeper sense of symbolism. This use, however, is not strictly accurate. Those churches known as sacramental churches maintain that a sacrament has power to save or to insure the

the church

inclusion of its communicant in the grace of Christ and the benefits of church connection. This is not what Baptists believe, whether or not they use the term.

ordinances

Historically, Baptists did not develop a theology of sacraments. Even among Baptists who use the term "sacrament" to describe the Lord's Supper and baptism, none assign to either one the power to effect salvation. Virtually all Baptist confessions and faith statements agree that baptism is an outward sign of an inward and invisible presence of grace. They agree that its proper form is done by immersion, not by aspersion (sprinkling) or imputation (pouring or touching), and that for it to represent the experience of salvation by one who is able to repent and willing to receive God's grace in Christ, it must be experienced by adults able to make a responsible decision, not by children.

As we have seen, this insistence upon adult baptism and the full immersion of the body as the appropriate means is what gained Baptists the name "Dunkards" on the European continent, and later in England the name "Baptists." It should be noted, however, that over the last century especially, many Baptists have participated in ceremonies of "infant dedication," a ritual that fulfills the appropriate desire of parents and congregation to celebrate the arrival of a new life and to participate in a commitment to providing for the child's spiritual nurture.

Baptists understand baptism not as a means of salvation but as an initiatory act and a statement of faith. As such, it admits a person both to the fellowship of the congregation and to participation in the table of the Lord's Supper. As a prerequisite to membership in the fellowship or body of the church, it is also frequently a requirement of Baptist churches that those who hold leadership office, vote, participate in determining church affairs, or serve as ministers must be baptized. The seriousness and weight of the opportunities opened by baptism therefore demands that, for Baptists, it be experienced only by those able to exercise their responsibility.

Likewise, Baptists generally tend to view the Lord's Supper as a memorial meal that recalls the presence of Christ with the disciples, and that serves to bind the fellowship of the church with the fellowship of Christ. As with baptism, the ritual is not understood to have redemptive qualities in itself.

Because partaking of the Lord's Supper is for Baptists a community act, Baptist practice does not encourage the Lord's Supper to be conducted in private or used as an exclusive bond, such as in a wedding ceremony or at the bedside of a sick person, unless the use of the ceremony is explicitly intended to convey or represent the presence and participation of the whole fellowship of the church.

Implicit in Baptist observance of the Lord's Supper ("Communion") is the recognition of the sacrificial character of Christ as the "lamb of God." Included also is its reminder of Jesus' own participation in the Passover meal, which gives it credence, on the night prior to his arrest. Its meaning, therefore, is especially bound up in the act of thanksgiving in memory of Christ's sacrificial death and in being a reminder of the expectation of Christ's return.

The Lord's Supper is also a celebration of the mutual love and support of the members of the church.[2] In that sense, it offers members an opportunity to remind themselves of their calling in Christ, both individually and corporately, and to recommit themselves to Christ's service. For that reason, many Baptists include the reading of a church covenant as a part of the observance of the Lord's Supper. It therefore is a way of proclaiming the gospel, but not a way of effecting salvation itself.

Because of the influences of other Christian traditions and the confusion that results for many who are not grounded in their Baptist heritage, there has been movement among Baptists away from historic emphases and practices as they pertain to the Lord's Supper. Many Baptist churches are home to persons raised in or familiar with the faith rituals of other denominations or churches, and many Baptist churches choose to diminish distinctions lest they prove divisive in the fellowship. As a result, although Baptists have no historical theology to support it, many churches do take Communion to hospitals and nursing homes and do perceive some individual value to receiving the elements of Communion in private.

It is likely that a more specific theology of the use of Communion for the sick or the lonely, or as a symbol of the presence of the fellowship of the church when the congregation is not fully present, will develop. Many Baptists already have extended participation in the Lord's Supper to guests and visitors by extending the invitation to participate to those of "like faith and order," leaving the definition of those who fit that category to self-interpretation. And, of course, many Baptists participate in the Communion rituals of other denominations or faith expressions at their own discretion.

Because the rise of the Baptist movement was roughly

congruent with the rise of the temperance movement in the United States and elsewhere, the use of wine in the celebration of the Lord's Supper has been replaced by many Baptists with the use of nonalcoholic grape juice. Some Baptists (and many of their critics) have noticed the anomaly of this adjustment in the face of clear scriptural precedent that suggests that wine was used in the communities of the New Testament. This practice, too, has been subject to some modification. Some Baptist churches have relaxed the prohibition on the use of alcohol for Communion and now provide both juice and wine, while churches from traditions accustomed to using wine have begun offering juice as an alternative out of sensitivity to those for whom exposure to alcohol may be damaging or objectionable.

Other rituals and ceremonies are often part of Baptist worship. Among these are services that commission persons to specific service in the church or in its mission, services of ordination to pastoral ministry or to certain offices in the church, and services that feature practices such as foot washing or healing. Baptist ministers also frequently solemnize marriages and lead services of memorial at times of death. All of these aspects of worship in the context of the faith community are greatly beneficial to the life of faith in the congregation, but historically none of these worship practices are recognized by Baptists as ordinances or sacraments. Thus, they have a secondary status in Baptist worship.

In sum, Baptists historically recognize only two ordinances. Baptism provides a powerful ritual of renewal, and the celebration of the Lord's Supper calls for a reflection on the meaning of Christ's death and a renewal of the participant's commitment.

ministry

The local church is also the center of ministry for Baptists. As is true of most Christian churches, specially designated (or ordained) professional ministers usually are authorized to lead in the administration of the affairs of the church, to plan and lead worship experiences, and to preach, teach, and provide pastoral care. Baptists generally have had high expectations of such designated or ordained ministers, especially regarding their roles as preacher and leader in the congregation.

But Baptist concepts of ministry also are shaped by the historic Baptist interpretation of the "priesthood of all believers" and by the democratic, autonomous character of local church life. From their earliest beginnings, Baptists rejected the idea of a class of priests to whom should be entrusted ultimate authority for biblical truth, sacramental leadership, or absolute executive power. In spiritual matters they earnestly believed that Christ was the only mediator between God and humankind, and they stoutly resisted any sense of need for prelates, synods, or hierarchies that might come between them and God.

Biblically and theologically, Baptists view ministry as the responsibility of the entire congregation, not just the clergy. While this ideal is not consistently realized in every church, it is a defining characteristic for Baptists. Every member is a priest and a servant in God's community of the faithful, and each possesses equal privileges and responsibilities within the life of the church.

Early Baptists sought, as much as possible, to pattern their churches after the model of New Testament churches. As there is biblical precedent for delegating responsibility within churches, most Baptists soon designated or ordained members to two special functions: pastors and deacons. In general, pastors were charged with leading the church in greater understanding of the word of God in Scripture, while deacons were charged with leading the church in clarifying church order and providing ministry in service to others. In fact, many Baptist churches ordained both pastors and deacons. Ordination, however, was not assumed to endow its recipients with special powers, prestige, or authority, but instead symbolized both the confidence and the expectation of the congregation in fulfilling their respective roles.

In most Baptist organizations, educational standards have been developed to encourage the successful service of ministers as preachers, teachers, and leaders in local congregations. In many Baptist denominations, basic educational requirements are a prerequisite to ordination to ministry. Likewise, although ordination among Baptists originally was perceived to be strictly a matter of the local church, in practice most ordinations are conducted in consultation with other churches or with denominational leaders, and those who are ordained often are recognized by their respective denomination as being among a professional class. This is an example of how Baptists have moderated some of their original views and principles.

The social developments of the last hundred years, especially, have encouraged a high degree of specialization in most careers and professions in the United States and elsewhere. It has been impossible for Baptist churches and institutions to resist the urge to more clearly designate roles and functions in ministry and leadership. Roles of leadership and service likewise have multiplied. Contemporary Baptist churches often specifically designate professional roles in areas of leadership or service in preaching, administration, youth ministry, counseling, and recreation.

Most Baptist denominations or associations have organized for the better support of missions and ministry, and to do so, have developed hierarchies of management as well. Those serving the purposes of these organizations carry titles such as "director," "executive minister," and other titles that imply ultimate responsibility, command, or, alternatively, specific responsibility for program or performance. Most Baptists, however, continue to resist the traditional terms of ecclesiastical hierarchy such as "bishop" or "canon."[3]

governance

Although Baptist churches are governed by congregational participation, it is not entirely accurate to state that congregational affairs are determined by democratic process. Whether in tackling matters such as church budgets and program priorities or in articulating spiritual goals, the Baptist tradition is to attempt to achieve a consensus by which church members are convinced that they are guided by the Holy Spirit in understanding the "mind of Christ" or the "will of God." The most successful Baptist decisions result when this state of universal understanding is reached. When consensus cannot be achieved, most Baptist churches provide that a majority will determine their direction. However, close or contested votes in Baptist churches often are warning signs of division or discontent, and therefore many churches will defer action until greater unanimity in spirit and intent can be achieved.

Pastoral leadership in congregational life is, therefore, a delicate job requiring both spiritual maturity and political savvy. In some Baptist churches, the pastor is designated as the moderator for church business meetings. In that role, the church may look to the pastor to guide them in a process of achieving decisions and directions on matters of concern. In other churches, the role of moderator is delegated to a layperson. In that case, the church may well look to the pastor for an opinion or position on matters of importance. Both styles of leadership have advantages and disadvantages. Effective pastoral leadership usually results when the pastor can model scriptural principles and build congregational unity. Problems generally occur when the congregation is unable or unwilling to respect the pastor's unique role as spiritual and organizational leader, or when there are differing expectations within a congregation regarding the role of the pastor. Difficulties may also occur, especially among Baptists, when a pastor confuses the need for leadership with his or her own desire for control.

Baptist churches have the potential to exhibit both the highest level of participatory decision-making and the lowest level of bitter dispute and division. Both results have their common origin in the local, independent, congregational character of Baptist traditions and beliefs about the church. There are two old adages that provide both a critique of Baptist failures and an implicit endorsement of the deep conviction of Baptist polity. The first is, "Baptists multiply by dividing." Baptist unity is a glorious thing, when it is evident. The fact that such unity frequently is absent is testimony to the powerful convictions that individual Baptists hold and to their willingness to express them and act upon them. The second adage is, "The history of the church is the best argument for the divine origin of the church;

no other organization could have survived the centuries of bad management." While this probably applies to all churches, Baptists especially have been characterized by debilitating conflict and debate within their congregations, although always with the confidence that in the end, God will direct and decide the future of God's own kingdom.

Despite the challenge of achieving unity in a participatory congregational life, Baptists are unanimous in acknowledging that the church is the body of Christ and belongs to Christ. Christ is its head and its leader. Christ is Lord of the church. It is in the doctrine of the church—its nature, worship, ordinance, ministry, and mission—that the essential characteristics for Baptist faith and life are demonstrated.

notes

1. William R. Estep, *Why Baptists? A Study of Baptist Faith and Heritage* (Dallas: Baptist General Convention of Texas, 1997), 30.

2. In recent years some Baptists have begun to use the term *Eucharist* in preference to *Lord's Supper* or *Communion*. Considerable resistance remains, however, because the word *Eucharist* implies a more exclusive spiritual communion with God, whereas Baptist tradition emphasizes that the Lord's Table is spiritual communion both with God and with one's fellow participants in faith in the local church.

3. Some Baptists do use terms such as *bishop*, however, preferring terms that are biblical or at least ancient in Christian use to the adoption of terms that reflect secular management models. The use of titles in Baptist church organizational and denominational structure is currently under active review by many Baptists and is one area in which diversity among Baptists is very apparent.

chapter 12

what makes baptists
baptist: freedom

A t first glance, it might seem that an emphasis on freedom
suggests that Baptists can believe anything. But such is
not the reality. A Baptist who does not believe that study and
interpretation of Scripture are important cannot be imagined,
nor can a Baptist who does not hunger for heartfelt worship.
Baptists also believe that personal behavior is important.

Baptists are independent and have a passion for freedom, but
they are not frivolous. In fact, Baptists inherited enough of the
spirit of their pietistic ancestors that they frequently (and sometimes justifiably!) are the subject of jokes about their stern
demeanor or their demanding ethics. With other Christians,
Baptists have at their core certain basic beliefs and assumptions
that are enormously important. But when it comes to defining
who Baptists really are, two concepts transcend all others. They
are freedom, which is the subject of this chapter, and mission,
the topic of the next chapter.

From their earliest origins, Baptists have advocated and cherished freedom in belief and worship, freedom in the interpretation of Scripture, freedom from interference by governmental

and religious authority, and even freedom to reject belief in God. Belief in freedom has sometimes cost individual Baptists dearly, and in every generation insistence on freedom tends to encourage disruption and even chaos in the organizational and institutional expressions of Baptist life. Nevertheless, freedom lies at the heart of what it means to be Baptist.

Freedom was a primary concern in the experience of the earliest Baptists, whether freedom from the authority of the historic Roman Catholic Church in sixteenth-century Europe or freedom from the established or reformed churches of England. It was at the heart of Roger Williams's protests against the Congregational established church in Massachusetts and was embedded in his leadership of the Baptist churches in Rhode Island, and even in establishing the colonial government of that state.

Freedom has tinged Baptist organizations with limits on their own authority, and has sometimes contributed to their inefficiency. The demand for freedom for slaves by some Baptists was the cause that drove other Baptists to form a new denomination. And those who left cited freedom as the reason for their leaving. The question of freedom has been at the heart of more recent Baptist controversies—freedom as it relates to such topics as denominational standards and directions, moral absolutes, and biblical authority. Baptist concepts of freedom can be broken into several broad categories.

soul freedom

In recent years, Baptists have reclaimed an expression used by some of their earliest ancestors: "soul freedom." With Christians of some other traditions, Baptists have advocated the idea of the "priesthood of all believers." That expression, used by some of the leaders of the Reformation, was a radical and formative concept. But freedom as understood and cherished by Baptists goes deeper into the fabric of faith and life; hence, the more comprehensive, though undoubtedly still inadequate, phrase "soul freedom" is more powerfully accurate.

In his 1908 book *Axioms of Religion,* Baptist teacher and scholar E. Y. Mullins characterized soul freedom as "the sinner's response to the gospel message as an act of moral freedom" or, more simply, "the capacity to deal directly with God." H. Wheeler Robinson, an observer and historian of Baptists in Britain in the early part of the twentieth century, suggested that soul freedom is the substance that connects all other important Baptist beliefs. For Robinson, soul freedom united the Baptist views that every individual has the right to a personal interpretation of and obedience to Scripture, that every person is free to encounter God directly and without mediation by any agency or personality, and that in politics, Baptists are committed to the separation of church and state in order that neither one could cripple the other.

When Baptists speak of soul freedom, they speak of a condition that feeds a deep hunger of people seeking authenticity, personal contact, and specific connections with God through faith. It is to this condition that Baptist faith has spoken.

Martin Luther King Jr. was a Baptist pastor and political activist who changed the course of history both in his own country and around the world. Specifically, King sought to rectify the deep injustices of racism, but he effected his change with words that spoke universally of freedom at the deepest level. Sitting in a jail cell in Birmingham, Alabama, after having been arrested on a variety of charges resulting from a demonstration, King wrote to his fellow clergy of his deep personal disappointment at their failure to respond. It was an eloquent letter, later to be published as "Letter from a Birmingham Jail," and at its heart were an affirmation—that all persons are called to be free—and a question.

The question was, "How can any be free as long as even one person is not?" And by implication he also asked, "How, then, are we connecting Scripture to life if we are not about making people free?" Several years later, this time standing in the very heart of the United States capital, he galvanized a nation when he said, "I have a dream," and in that dream described freedom in prophetic, biblical terms. On his headstone are inscribed the words "Free at Last! Thank God Almighty, Free at Last!" King's power was rooted in his understanding of soul freedom. It connected even with many of his harshest critics.

Soul freedom puts the individual front and center in human experience. For Baptists, the story of God's creation comes to its fullest meaning in Genesis 1:26, in which God says, "Let us make humankind in our image." Being created in the image and likeness of God, each individual is, in Baptist belief, competent, privileged, and responsible to make moral, spiritual, and religious decisions. Naturally, such a view contributes to a strong tradition of individualism, which, as we have seen, sometimes has created division. Nevertheless, Baptists have remained true to the principle of freedom.

Some traditions conclude that faith comes to its highest fruition in the church. Others see religion as a matter of right belief, an expression of the mind. Still others understand an approach to God as a matter of confession and creed. Baptists believe that all these things are secondary.

Instead, Baptists understand the first and most important relationship with God as a matter of the heart—an individual connection. Walter Shurden, who has written extensively on Baptist principles, suggests that Jesus' question to Peter in Matthew 16:15 shapes Baptist responses. At first, in Matthew 16:13, Jesus asked, "Who do people say that the Son of Man is?" Peter responded, "Some say John the Baptist, but others Elijah, and still others Jeremiah or one of the prophets." Contemporary Christians sometimes find it disconcerting that it was not obvious who Jesus was, even to his closest colleagues. But as Shurden argues, the whole point of Jesus and his ministry was contained in a free and personal response to this question.[1]

Baptists have a profound appreciation for spiritual life as a member of a faith community, but they emphasize that it begins in the individual in personal response, or "conversion," in the presence of God. For Baptists, soul freedom means that a person is not a church member by birth, tradition, or assumption, but by conviction. It is voluntary, but more than that, soul freedom is a choice. Baptists have strong convictions about how they came to believe and strong memories about their own first encounter with God. Sometimes they err by assuming that all others have experienced the presence of God in the same way they have. But when pressed, Baptists are passionate that each person encounters Christ and expresses faith in his or her own way. For some, it is a dramatic moment never forgotten, just like Paul's encounter with Christ on the Damascus road. For others, it is a moment of dawning spiritual enlightenment that grows in intensity and complexity as it penetrates the fullness of life.

Throughout their history, Baptists periodically have had to rediscover this overarching principle of soul freedom. From time to time, some Baptists have asserted that salvation depends on having the right belief. Others have asserted that being a Baptist depends on having the right style of worship, singing the right hymns, or engaging in the right activities. Still others have sought to demonstrate a particular "Baptist way" in a prescribed pattern of behavior or even political ideology. But in each such case, the overwhelming tide of Baptist sentiment and passion has reasserted the reality of soul freedom, with its individualism and personalism.

Soul freedom perhaps is illustrated most clearly in the Baptist concept of baptism. For Baptists, as for many Christians, baptism is a formal ritual by which faith is expressed and a desire to publicly follow Christ is announced. Baptists received their name, of course, because of their peculiar method of baptism by immersion.[2] But the particular manner of baptism is not what distinguishes Baptists; rather, it is the timing and meaning of it. In some Christian expressions, baptism represents the acceptance of a person, often an infant or child, into the community of faith, with the expectation that at some later date the person will affirm the faith. In others, baptism is a sacrament that implies entry into God's presence. For Baptists, however, baptism is a ritual only for believers who have experienced God's presence, who have determined as a matter of conviction to express their faith in God, and who have decided to state that faith in a public way through baptism. In other words, baptism is perceived as the result of a personal, free, and voluntary choice based on personal conviction.

This does not mean Baptists ought not be a part of the larger, universal church or that Baptists have nothing to learn from others. But as C. Brownlow Hastings put it in a book written largely to introduce Southern Baptists to Roman Catholics,

> I may study the Bible under great teachers and share with devoted Christian friends, but I must finally judge what is truth, not because I find it agreeable to me, but because the inner witness of the Spirit convinces me. I may profit by the testimony of another's experience in the Lord, but I do not need and cannot repeat his experience. I need my own.[3]

It is this need and a desire to fulfill it that describes soul freedom.

religious freedom

Early Baptists had to struggle against both tradition and established laws governing religious expression in order to worship and believe as their conscience directed them. Therefore, from their earliest origins, Baptists have both deeply cherished and fiercely asserted the principle of religious freedom, sometimes more specifically referred to as the "separation of church and state."

Roger Williams wrote, "To call a nation a 'Christian Nation' may make a nation of hypocrites; but it will not make one single true believer." John Leland, Revolutionary-era Baptist leader, said shrewdly, "The fondness of magistrates to foster Christianity has done it more harm than all the persecutions ever did."[4]

The Baptist view of religious liberty—"separation of church and state" or, as it is also sometimes identified, "freedom of conscience"—is deeply rooted in biblical principles, in personal and practical experience, and, in fact, in sympathy with a great many political philosophers from the sixteenth century until now. From a biblical perspective, Baptists do not argue so much from a particular text as from an understanding that it is of the very nature of God's creation of humankind for people to be free, and that it is of the very nature of humankind, from the earliest stories of creation, to make decisions of their own— even if such decisions turn out to be flawed or wrong.

Baptist ministers, lay leaders, and others throughout Baptist history have regularly upheld the principles of freedom of speech and religious practice, even when in so doing they raised the ire of colleagues who could not understand why, on a critical issue of moral principle or policy, men and women of Baptist conviction would defend the rights of their opponents to disagree. It has, in fact, created for Baptists some strange allies as they have gone to court or spoken publicly in defense of people who were advocating positions or practices that they, as Baptists, personally found offensive.

This dynamic is common among Baptists today. In the last generation, a great many Christians have found it tempting to advocate legislation that would require certain behaviors consistent with their beliefs or would restrict other behaviors that were not. Many self-identified Baptists have been at the forefront of movements to legislate specifically in areas of human life, medical ethics and treatment, or to restrict the publication of certain materials, particularly those related to human sexuality and behavior or to ideas inconsistent with majority religious views. A recent proposal to use federal funding to support outreach programs sponsored by "faith-based communities" that alleviate human suffering has become particularly controversial in the religious community. Although Baptists are committed to the relief of human suffering, they are deeply suspicious of the end result of such government-funded programs.

The reason for this fierce defense of principle is that deep within their souls—at that point where soul freedom is alive—Baptists understand that when the rights of anyone are compromised, particularly the right to express and practice religious belief, their own spiritual integrity is compromised, and their understanding of God's intention for personal freedom is breached.

For Baptists, the idea of freedom in religious expression and practice is fundamentally very personal. But they have understood that its health and protection can be truly guaranteed only by keeping the boundaries between government and religious life clear. Thus, Baptists have historically demanded that the church and the state, however sympathetic, cordial, or united in purpose they might be, maintain a strict distance from one another.

For the church, this means refraining from any attempt to use the power of government to enhance the power or programs of a church. For the state, it means refraining from any attempt to govern the affairs of churches or from supporting any particular religious activity. It is, to be sure, a matter of great complexity, particularly in regions or nations such as in the United States, where a variety of religions and beliefs live in common community. In an age in which diversity is a constant challenge, on the other hand, it may be the Baptists' most valuable contribution to community understanding and peace.

scriptural freedom

Baptists have always been a Bible-believing people. But there is no such thing as a "Baptist translation" of the Bible. In fact, the Bible-based practices and beliefs of Baptists are similar at many points to those of other Christian traditions.

What, then, is unique about a Baptist sense of "scriptural freedom"? Early Christians struggled to formulate creeds that could help them define their belief and understand authority. Some Christians have looked to the authority of a church hierarchy, or a tradition, or both. (The Roman Catholic Church is one good example.)

Other Christians have sought spiritual authority in some sense of an indwelling, enlightening spirit that guides both individuals and gathered congregations in matters of faith and belief. In very different ways, both Quakers and charismatic Christians represent this approach. Still others, including many churches that came out of the Reformation, have recognized the Bible as their authority. *Sola scriptura* ("by Scripture alone") was, after all, a maxim of the Reformation period.

Indeed, Baptists are responsive to their leadership and traditions, have a strong sense of the Holy Spirit moving in them and among them in their church life, and certainly believe in the Bible as an unparalleled guide to life in faith. Baptists, however, recognize their ultimate authority in the power and presence of Jesus Christ. In all things, therefore, even including their use of Scripture, Baptists look to what they commonly understand as the "Lordship of Jesus Christ" as the guide. For Baptists in general, then, both the person and the spiritual presence of Jesus Christ are the standard by which the Bible should be interpreted. Most Baptists believe that "Jesus is Lord" was the first and most passionate confession of the early church.[5] Of course, it is Scripture itself that points Baptists to this assertion, but it is the general and overall presence of the historical Christ and the continuing presence of the fellowship of Christ as the living Lord that open biblical interpretation for individual Baptists.

Southern Baptists, who in recent years have engaged in considerable controversy over the exact nature of the inspiration, meaning, and authority of Scripture, wrote in their "Statement of the Baptist Faith and Message" in 1963, "Baptists are a people who profess a living faith. This faith is rooted and grounded in Jesus Christ who is 'the same yesterday, and today and forever.' Therefore, the sole authority for faith and practice among Baptists is Jesus Christ whose will is revealed in the Holy Scriptures." That is, the Bible is a dynamic book written with authority and fraught with meaning in the moment of scriptural authorship, but it is not a book buried in the past. It is a resource of faith that has new and unfolding meaning in the present and in the future.

The Southern Baptists, in that same 1963 statement, went on to say, "A living faith must experience a growing understanding of truth and must be continually interpreted and related to the needs of each new generation." This view of Scripture, sometimes referred to as the "Gainsborough Principle," is the oldest and most enduring Baptist view of the Bible, and it undergirds the principle of freedom by which individuals in faith approach its contents.

Baptists believe that individuals must be free to wrestle with biblical truth and to interpret it as their obedience to the living Lord directs them. It is, of course, a great challenge, particularly in a time when many Baptists, like many others, are familiar with very little of the Bible's actual contents.

Baptists today face a particular challenge in their understanding of biblical freedom. As we have seen, beginning in the nineteenth century, many challenges arose from the scientific and theological worlds to the authority of Scripture and the validity of traditional interpretations and understandings. The twentieth century was marked by conflicts between traditionalists, or fundamentalists, and others who favored the adoption of new standards for biblical interpretation.

The "battle for the Bible," as some called it, was particularly fierce among Baptists. On the one hand, Baptists until that time had proudly defended the individual's right to interpret Scripture. On the other hand, most Baptists agreed on broad and general issues of scriptural meaning. As the culture at large began to differ broadly in its comprehension of science, history, and other categorizations of human experience, significant differences also developed among Baptists in their understanding about how the Bible was inspired, written, and interpreted.

Many Baptists still agreed on the freedom of the individual to interpret Scripture, but only to a point. Some Baptists began to assert that in order to be Baptist, one had to believe certain things about the Bible and, specifically, other things contained in the Bible. Others insisted that to demand agreement on any point of belief, biblical or otherwise, would mean that Baptists were establishing a creed—something that Baptists had never done as a test for faith and orthodoxy.

Common issues of disagreement included whether the world was created in a seven-day period, as a literal reading of the Bible suggested, or whether it was a longer period of time, as science suggested. Was humankind created completely and exclusively in Adam and Eve, or were there others? Was humankind created in its present form, or did it evolve, as Darwin theorized? Were the great biblical stories about Moses, David, Elijah, and the people of Israel literally and historically true, or were they mythological (i.e., partly fabricated or embellished stories told to demonstrate a particular truth or purpose)? Were the Bible's assertions about the nature of sin and separation from God accurate, or were they simply ancient insights into human character, as psychology claimed? Was the Bible divinely inspired in some direct and personal way by God, or was it simply the product of human hands and therefore greatly diminished in authority, however inspired it might seem to be?

These were issues of great significance to all Christians, particularly Christians for whom the Bible was as important as or more important than traditions, creeds, or church authority. For many Baptists, however, the crisis was even more acute. By implication, a challenge to the Bible's nature and authority ultimately questioned the role of Jesus as the Christ. In what way was he truly the Son of God? How might he be an agent of human salvation? Was he sent by God to save the lost? Was he divinely conceived and grace-filled for that purpose? Or, was Jesus of Nazareth simply a man of unique characteristics who possessed a strong sense of mystery and developed keen spiritual insights, as some biblical critics proposed? If so, in what way could Baptists believe Jesus Christ was a "living Lord"?

Fundamentalism and its related sympathizers passed through the twentieth century in waves, eventually creating schism or disturbance in many denominations. Among Baptists in the North, debate over biblical authority was the flash point of denominational division in the 1930s and 1940s. In the South, generally a more biblically conservative region, fundamentalism exercised a profound popular influence in the 1920s but reemerged in nearly every decade, especially the early 1960s. Then, with particular strength, in a form of "authoritative biblicism" that often seemed to exalt the Bible as an authority even above Jesus Christ, it erupted in the Southern Baptist Convention in the early 1980s.

While the eventual ramifications of that era are yet uncertain, it is clear that one line of division had to do with freedom of interpretation. Extreme biblical conservatives insisted on agreement in interpretation and on the "inerrant" inspiration of the Bible. Others, including many with widely divergent opinions on specific issues, often called "moderates," reasserted their belief in the Bible and its inspired resources but insisted that ultimately each person was by right and by responsibility bound to interpret Scripture personally.

These issues centered on biblical freedom have engulfed virtually every Baptist body. The American Baptist Churches in the USA, the Baptist body most directly continuing the early Baptist traditions, and sometimes considered more centrist, or even liberal, by some other Baptists, has been occupied with similar debate for over a decade. Surface issues often have been

defined around the role of women in ministry or church leadership, or more heatedly, around the question of whether
homosexuality is biblically or spiritually acceptable, especially in
the person of a minister. But the underlying issue often is centered on the interpretation of Scripture: whether there is one
clear truth in every important circumstance, or whether in
many things individual or communal interpretation is open to
divergence and disagreement. It is fair to say that among Baptists, every debate about biblical authority or meaning is in reality a debate about freedom of interpretation.

It is impossible at present to fully interpret the long-term
effect and result of many specific issues in the life of Baptist
organizations and among Baptist people. It is certain, however,
that the long-held Baptist principle of freedom in biblical interpretation is at the center of present Baptist life. And its presence
is a very important cause of the frequently observed presence of
conflict among Baptists. Thus far, it has been the judgment of
history that Baptists ultimately grow and increase from such
freedom, and that it is, in fact, part of their creative dynamic.

notes
1. Shurden, *Baptist Identity,* 25.
2. Baptism by immersion is asserted by many, especially Baptists, to be biblical.
It is, in fact, historical, having been practiced, and probably preferred, by early
Christians for the first centuries of the church. By the time of Baptist beginnings
in the sixteenth century, however, it was a radical expression in comparison to
baptism by aspersion (sprinkling), which was practiced by most of the Christian
churches of the time.
3. C. Brownlow Hastings, *Introducing Southern Baptists: Their Faith and Their
Life* (New York: Paulist Press, 1981), 24. Cited in Shurden, *Baptist Identity,* 31.
4. Cited in James M. Dunn's address to the American Baptist Churches in the
USA 2001 biennial meeting.
5. See, for example, Romans 10:9; Philippians 2:11.

chapter 13

what makes baptists baptist: outreach and mission

The spirit of freedom often divides Baptists. The purpose of mission unites them. Whereas many varied efforts to achieve Baptist unity have failed, the work of missions is the one activity around which Baptist individuals and organizations have unified.

baptist missions: chapters in the story

Quite apart from the early "foreign" mission activities exemplified in America especially by Adoniram Judson and Luther Rice, Baptists had become a dynamic and growing movement at home as they entered the nineteenth century. The Great Awakening, as earlier suggested, infused Baptists with new life and new people. It also energized Baptist individuals and churches with enthusiasm to share their faith experience.

Even Baptist churches from educated or sophisticated traditions often experienced cycles of spiritual awakening and dynamic outreach that resulted in growth. In 1795, Stephen Gano and Isaac Backus, two Baptist leaders of reflection and intellectual substance, led New England Baptist ministers in a "circular letter" calling upon churches to pray for revival. In 1803 the First Baptist Church of Boston, which had opposed George Whitefield's revivalism sixty years earlier, experienced a remarkable period of revitalization.

Farther west and in the South, evangelism, revivals, and a passion for sharing a revitalized, personal gospel led to waves of revival activity, camp meetings, and extraordinary numbers of baptisms. Although revival meetings often appeared to be spontaneous and the result of a sudden visitation by the Holy Spirit, most often they were the result of careful planning and work. Baptists frequently participated in the revivals and other gatherings organized by Presbyterians or Methodists.

Baptist revivals tended to be focused in a particular church or were sponsored specifically by a church or association. During a particularly intense period of revivals between 1790 and 1830, for example, Baptists in New York State grew from four thousand (1790) to twelve thousand (1800) to sixty thousand (1832). Individual churches with memberships of a hundred or so often reported dozens, sometimes even a hundred or more, new baptisms as the result of sponsoring a revival or participating with other churches in a regional evangelistic effort.[1]

However, Baptists were never fully convinced that large-scale revivalism, with its temptation to emotional excess and physical demonstration, was a preferred method of outreach. Early on, therefore, Baptists relied on the establishment of church programs such as Sunday schools and formal educational institutions to help shape and encourage a Christian life and spirit in their young people and to insure the proper training of ministers. In addition to the college already established in Rhode Island in the middle of the eighteenth century, later named Brown University, Baptists created and developed an astonishing number of schools, academies, colleges, universities, and seminaries in the first half of the nineteenth century. Just a few examples include the Newton Theological Institution (now Andover Newton Theological School), Columbian College in Washington, D.C. (later redeveloped and now continuing as George Washington University), and academies that later were to develop into Colby College, Hamilton College, Kalamazoo College, and Franklin College in the North, and Mercer University, the University of Richmond, Georgetown College, and Wake Forest University in the South, to name just a few.

After 1850 Baptist commitment to education continued, with the ultimate effect of creating a wealth of institutions of higher education in every region of the country. Among the institutions that Baptists nurtured are several—including Baylor University in the South, the University of Chicago in the North, and others—that have developed regional, national, or international reputations for excellence in education and research. Baptists were responsible for founding or nurturing several institutions dedicated to providing education for freed slaves, including Spelman College and Morehouse College, both in Atlanta. Baptists also founded Bacone College in Oklahoma, established for Native Americans.[2]

Despite the long and enduring impact of the educational institutions they created, Baptist outreach and mission perhaps were most effectively carried out in the nineteenth century through the work of Sunday schools and by the distribution of educational and inspirational literature through a powerful distribution network that in itself became a mission enterprise.

Baptists were, in fact, the first, or at least among the first, to establish Sunday schools in the United States.[3] Although there likely were some earlier formal efforts at religious education, Sunday schools seem to have been established first in 1791 in Philadelphia, Providence, and Passaic Falls (New Jersey). Sunday schools quickly gained popularity, and by 1824 many participated in the creation of the American Sunday School Union. The earliest of these schools sought to address the need for basic education for urban and rural people who either had no access to education or had no time available to devote to it.

In many of these early programs the focus was on the "three Rs." But the possibility for evangelism and outreach quickly became apparent. Particularly in the frontier areas Sunday schools were an effective method of bringing a rudimentary understanding of the Bible and religion at the same time that basic education was offered, and such Sunday schools often preceded and made possible the establishment of a church.

With the establishment and success of the Sunday school movement there arose a need for specialized materials to supply curriculum needs and, related to that, a need for an effective method of distributing the materials. In 1824 the Baptist General Tract Society was organized in Washington, D.C.—a forerunner of the American Baptist Publication Society. Its key leaders included its president, Obadiah B. Brown, president of Columbian College and pastor of First Baptist Church in Washington; and its treasurer, Luther Rice. By 1826 the Society's board voted to move to Philadelphia, which was the center for printing and publication, and in 1827 they published their first periodical.[4] Very soon, urgent calls for materials from churches on the frontiers in the West and likewise from those serving in mission posts overseas defined a need for even more general publication. In 1840 the Baptist General Tract Society became the American Baptist Publication and Sunday School Society. Soon the Society was publishing a variety of materials for evangelism, education, mission outreach, worship, and music.

Following their departure in 1845 from the national gatherings at the Triennial Conventions, the Southern Baptists likewise made the establishment of Sunday schools and the publication of materials a priority. In 1854 Kentucky Baptists were concerned about the nondenominational character of the literature published by the American Sunday School Union; their concern resulted in the establishment of the Southern Baptist Publication Society and, later, the Southern Sunday School Union in Memphis. By 1863 a Sunday School Board was created by the Southern Baptist Convention, which later was merged with the Southern Baptist Publication Society. Following the Civil War, the Convention ultimately established a new organization to continue the work of the Sunday School Board and located it in Nashville. Among Southern Baptists, the publication of increasingly vast amounts of literature and an emphasis on the founding and support of Sunday schools were key to the rapid growth and success in establishing Southern Baptist churches in the South and the West.

By the middle of the nineteenth century, immigration and the new churches and Sunday schools that followed it had challenged the distribution ability of the American Baptist Publication

Society. Distribution routes were undefined and in many cases nonexistent. Also, many of the churches and Sunday schools did not have pastors or consistent leadership of any kind. The Society therefore developed a strategy that employed traveling missionaries known as colporters, who carried Bibles, denominational tracts, and other materials and books to Sunday schools and churches and to individuals in remote or sparsely populated regions. These missionaries often were the only link that isolated people had to the outside world, and their materials the only windows into the experiences of others and the only doorways to knowledge, religious or otherwise. As the effectiveness of their ministry and mission became apparent, colporters were encouraged to establish Sunday schools where none existed. Late in the nineteenth century the work of colporters was expanded by the development of "chapel cars." Railroad chapel cars were outfitted as mobile "minichurches," with living quarters for itinerant missionaries and their families. In some cases they also carried additional supplies for colporters, who then would receive and deliver the materials to settlements and towns beyond the railheads.[5] Still later, as the Pacific Northwest and Alaska were developed, boats were used similarly to deliver materials and provide missionary contact with towns and cities in Puget Sound and along the coast of Alaska.

Baptist missions in North America frequently were intertwined with education and publication concerns, but they were not totally defined by those activities. In the early nineteenth century Baptists commissioned missionaries to the American frontier and others to work in Burma and elsewhere. John Mason Peck, for example, was assigned to the Missouri Territory and began his work around St. Louis in 1817. Peck was an effective and energetic missionary, and either by his direct leadership or as a result of his encouragement and pressure for support from the newly developed American Baptist Home Mission Society, he established a church in St. Louis and established fifty public schools in remote settlements, created a system for collecting funds in support of missions, and helped to support a missionary to the Native Americans in the Wabash region. Peck's sturdy determination and effectiveness were evident in many other men and women working in missions.

However, regionalism often retarded both enthusiasm and support for the work that Peck and the Home Mission Society envisioned. Antimission sentiment was strong in some areas of the Midwest and the West, and resentment toward leadership from the East existed as well. Nevertheless, the work of the Home Mission Society persisted, and by century's end they had developed programs of support and encouragement for struggling congregations to assist in designing and constructing church buildings, training pastors, and promoting evangelism among newly arriving immigrants, including Scandinavians, Germans, Italians, and many others in lesser numbers from other language and cultural backgrounds.

Southern Baptists, meanwhile, also commissioned missionaries through a Board of Domestic Missions, first located in Marion, Alabama. Nineteenth-century priorities included evangelism among Native Americans and African Americans, and they targeted especially the city of New Orleans, which was the strategic population center at the gateway of the Mississippi River. Southern Baptists assumed, probably correctly, that to stunt the rival growth of Roman Catholicism at that gateway would help to insure strong Baptist witness in the lower Mississippi region and determine the faith expression of much of the South and the Southwest. During the latter half of the century Southern Baptists continued to expand their work in both the settled areas and the new territories, eventually establishing missions in several locations in Central America.

At the close of the Civil War there were several moments when Baptists from the North and the South promoted the idea of reunion and renewed cooperation in missions and evangelism, particularly in the United States. Baptists from the North, in fact, continued to assist churches and missions in the South, but their activities met continued suspicion and resentment. Proposals for reunion, therefore, invariably incurred bitterness and disagreement, and ultimately leaders from both regions assumed that it was better to hope that time would heal their divisions. This hope, sadly, has never been fulfilled. However, in the latter part of the twentieth century, divisions among Baptists, especially within the Southern Baptist Convention, related to issues of authority and biblical interpretation had the ultimate effect of bringing many former Southern Baptist "moderates" into closer association and common purpose with Baptists elsewhere. The twenty-first century may yet see a unification of many Baptists in North America.

While Baptist missions, evangelism, and education shared in the dynamic development of new territories and regions in North America, missions abroad also expanded with remarkable force. In Burma, for example, the Baptists' first "mission field," progress had been remarkable. By 1855 there were nine mission stations in Burma, five of which opened between 1853 and 1855. New mission locations continued to open in subsequent decades, and by 1900 forty-seven of Burma's tribes had contact with Baptist missions, and there were nearly fifty thousand church members, the majority being from the Karen people.[6] In less than a century, a very significant beginning had been accomplished for Baptists in southeastern Asia.

In India, too, Baptists had been able to continue the work begun by William Carey. The people of Assam, especially hill people such as the Garos and the Molungs, responded with cordiality and interest to missionary efforts, and in some cases whole villages accepted Christianity as a result. The most dramatic response, however, was in Telugus at Ongole, India. In 1835 the Triennial Convention had heard of the need of the Telugu people south of Orissa. Almost immediately a mission effort was established there, and eventually its headquarters was located in Nellore. Several missionaries located in the region, and in the early years their results were quite discouraging. By 1875 to 1876, however, in the midst of famine in the region, the persistence of the preaching, teaching, and compassion of the missionaries resulted in several startling periods of commitment. On Christmas morning of 1877 almost 2,300 persons were baptized. By 1879 the number of new Christians resulting from the mission work in this area had reached 10,500.[7]

A new focus of Baptist missions in the latter part of the nineteenth century was in Africa, particularly in the region of the Congo. American Baptist missions continued in Liberia, but in 1856 leadership was transferred to the Southern Baptists. Later, Liberian missions were continued primarily by African American leadership, while the Southern Baptists focused on Yoruba on the Niger River. In the Congo, meanwhile, by 1900, following a revival period similar to that among the Karens in Burma and the Telugus of India, there were more than 1,500 church members led by fifty-seven African preachers and teachers, mostly affiliated with three large churches.

Another growing field was in China, where chapels and hospitals were established in five of the "open ports" and interior centers of evangelism were set up under American Baptist Missionary Union auspices. By 1900 the work established at Swatow had become self-supporting, and the Bible had been translated into the Swatow and Nigpo dialects. In Shanghai, as a result of missionaries sponsored by the Southern Baptist Foreign Mission Board, the church was strong enough that by 1874 the First Baptist Church of Shanghai was contributing over eight hundred dollars annually to the Southern Baptist Convention. By 1900 the Southern Baptists had organized in three Chinese fields twenty-four churches and thirty-six additional outstations. Church membership approached 2,300, and their thirty-four schools enrolled over nine hundred students.

By 1900 what had begun as a visionary mission by a handful of committed and faithful young Baptists symbolized by Adoniram Judson had become a global enterprise, with Baptist missions organized and expanding on every continent and into a number of the island civilizations of the world. Even the Middle East and Europe, respectively the birthplace and the cradle of Christianity, became fertile ground for the uniquely personal evangelism and fervent purpose of Baptist missionaries.

Two broad themes had begun to emerge for Baptist missions

abroad. The first was that unlike mission emphases in the United States, which used the formation of schools and Sunday schools as a primary strategy, missions abroad, especially those under American Baptist Missionary Union leadership, increasingly gave preaching and personal evangelism highest priority. As a result, Baptists beyond the United States tended to become very specifically evangelical and conversion oriented. It also enabled Baptists to be effective in encouraging the growth of their churches and mission stations by encouraging committed new membership.

A second theme, the result of a clear policy decision among many Baptists, was that of developing self-supporting, indigenous churches. In 1895 the American Baptist Missionary Union reported that the number of self-supporting Baptist churches in mission field areas had increased from 377 to 458 in one year, and the number of self-supporting schools from 247 to 369. Later, by reasserting the concept of indigenous leadership and of partnership between American and native missionary leaders, mission churches gained considerable strength. It was enough, in a remarkable number of cases, to enable them to survive two major world conflicts, during which time indigenous churches were cut off from support, leadership, or even communication from their previous mentors and partners. In China, churches survived not only World War II, but also several decades of oppression by a hostile authoritarian government. Missionaries under the auspices of the American Baptist Churches in the USA continued to strongly develop the partnership concept of missions after World War II.

baptist missions: the big picture

The specific chapters of the story of Baptist missions are numerous and their story powerful. In general, Baptist missions, along with the missions and outreach efforts of many other Christian bodies, have been criticized at times for seeming to be part of an imperialistic American approach to other parts of the world, or for failing to be sensitive in all cases to indigenous cultures and value systems, or for failing to confront matters of injustice, oppression, or inequality within the host country of their work. Some of these criticisms undoubtedly are accurate. Nevertheless, Baptist missions played a significant transforming role in the creation of the concept of "global community" that essentially is taken for granted now in the early years of the twenty-first century. Furthermore, from teachers to healers to preachers, Baptist missions and missionaries not only addressed personal, spiritual, and physical needs, but also created a worldwide network of idealists and visionaries who possessed a profound and realistic understanding of the need for connection and communication among all people and a sensitivity to cultural differences and their impact on culture and life. With characteristic purpose, Baptist missions went out to save souls, but as they traversed the rivers and highways of their work, they contributed to transforming the world.

For Baptists, with few exceptions, the doing of missions is the highest and holiest of work. We have noted that in general Baptist growth was most significant among ordinary people—those of meager financial means and, often, limited educational background. It is nothing less than extraordinary, therefore, to recognize that the impulse to evangelize and serve the whole world was empowered by resources of modest origins. Mission offerings, "widow's mites," children's penny collections—every imaginable fundraising effort and astonishing examples of personal sacrifice—established the support of mission activity much more often than did the checks of wealthy individuals.

In evaluating the role of Baptist missions, therefore, something of a double benefit becomes evident. The result of the missions per se can be judged on their collective merits. But within the life of Baptist churches, fellowships, and associations, the role of being inspired by and supporting missions cannot be overstated. In missions, the fellowship of Christ becomes real for Baptists. Aged cynics have regained a sense of commitment, and youthful idealists have found a focus for their lives. Children, hearing of the work of missionaries in faraway places, have discovered a new perspective on the world. Diplomats and government leaders all over the globe have acknowledged that their first interest in the affairs of people elsewhere was kindled by contact with missionaries or by learning about missions. Doing missions holds Baptists together. Cantankerous adversaries in congregations put aside their grudges to enlist their friends in support of missions; congregations regain a sense of their purpose when missionary speakers address them; associations and, at times, whole denominations step back from the brink of division or schism in order not to sacrifice their missions.

For early Baptists, to be a missionary was to walk with God. Much of that spirit remains. For many Baptists, to support a missionary is to be, like Peter the disciple, one upon whom the church of the future is being built. To speak of a missionary, especially one who has endured suffering, privation, or hardship and has prevailed, is to utter the name of a saint. Of course, Baptists do not believe in formalized saints any more than they do sacraments.

notes

1. Robert G. Torbet, *A History of the Baptists,* 3d ed. (Valley Forge, Pa.: Judson Press, 1963), 301.

2. Baptist individuals also frequently played key roles in the establishment of educational institutions that did not have any formal relationship to Baptist organizations. For example, Howard University in Washington, D.C., originally was conceived and begun by a group of prominent Baptists in the District of Columbia as a place of education for free Africans. Its name ultimately was taken in gratitude for a gift of money from a member of another denomination, and early in its establishment it became a public university that has served well its original vision by becoming a premier educational institution that historically has attracted a high proportion of African American students. Several of those who developed the founding vision for this university were trustees of Washington's First Baptist Church, and also were responsible for the creation of several of the capital's enduring charitable institutions, hospitals, and organizations.

3. English Methodists generally are credited with the establishment of the Sunday school movement in response to the plight of working children in England's industrialized cities. The establishment of the movement in the United States seems to have followed the same instinct and purpose by beginning in the first and most industrialized cities of the Eastern seaboard. The Second Baptist Church of Baltimore frequently is credited with the first Sunday school organized specifically and exclusively for educational purposes. See Torbet, *History of the Baptists,* 325.

4. One historian notes as an interesting sidelight that Luther Rice objected to the move to Philadelphia because he envisioned establishing Washington as the national location for all Baptist agencies. See Torbet, *History of the Baptists,* 326.

5. The story of the chapel cars is one of the most dramatic and interesting stories of Baptist mission outreach. See Wilma Rugh Taylor and Norman Thomas Taylor, *This Train Is Bound for Glory: The Story of America's Chapel Cars* (Valley Forge, Pa.: Judson Press, 1999).

6. Torbet, *History of the Baptists,* 340–41.

7. Ibid., 341–42.

CONCLUSION

baptists in the new millennium

Baptists today disagree among themselves about many of the same issues that divide the society at large: the roles of women, relations between and among races and cultures, diversity in sexual identity, the priorities of public policy—to name but a few. Throughout their history Baptists have also battled one another on important theological issues and on trivial ones. They have organized, reorganized, and then reorganized again. In short, they have been true to themselves and to the nature of Baptist identity.

Yet, whenever Baptists get together for meetings, conventions, revivals, worship, or a demonstration march for any of a variety of causes, when someone begins to sing a hymn, they all join in. Their hymns and songs and testimonies have become the informal creeds and confessions of a common experience and a passionate faith. Despite their sometimes painful divisions, Baptists inevitably sense their kinship and connection with one another and with the God they worship.

As Baptists travel through the third millennium, no one can predict with any accuracy how the years and experiences ahead will shape Baptist life or how Baptists will shape the future.

There are, however, several trends that clearly identify an emerging agenda.

First, diversity continues to change and disrupt virtually every established cultural pattern and institution everywhere in the world, especially in North America, where Baptists are strongest. As we have seen, Baptists have tended to adjust well to changing circumstances in the past, and they likely will continue to do so in the future. Change, however, also has intensified the inclination of Baptists to disagree and thus has sparked debate and division. We might safely predict that Baptists will continue to be noisy, frequently conflicted, and sometimes chaotic in dealing with diversity.

Second, a general declining sense of loyalty to many cultural and community habits and traditions has characterized some responses to change, while a hardening of definitions and practices has characterized others. Given Baptists' deep-rooted penchant for independence and local freedom of expression and practice, this dynamic may well erode any common or universal sense of what being Baptist means. It also may indicate that various strains of Baptists will exhibit remarkably different traditions and practices in developing their future styles of worship, patterns of witness, and occasions for fellowship.

Third, a trend of declining numbers of participants in established churches at the same time that new church organizations and religious expressions are being established for spiritual connection and fellowship will be particularly challenging for Baptists. Historically, Baptists have been especially successful in attracting people who wanted something different from traditional religious structures. Because Baptists have strongly established themselves at the center of American culture, at least, they are not now perceived as either radical or different. They are, instead, part of the religious "establishment" in many, if not most, important respects.

Fourth, Baptist identification with biblical literalism, fundamentalism, or absolutist views of faith, social ethics, or personal moral standards may create barriers for many people, especially in the aftermath of the traumatic attacks of September 11, 2001. To the degree that any kind of fundamentalist orientation, especially religious fundamentalism, is commonly perceived to lead to conflict or violence, those who profess such views may be increasingly marginalized in American life. At present, it seems that reasonableness, accommodation, toleration, mutual respect, and an insistence on dialogue rather than harsh debate or passionate persuasion will characterize the foreseeable future. Baptists possess both sets of characteristics, and so they will need to select carefully the principles of faith expression that will identify them as part of a positive national and global progress in shaping their future.

Fifth, the growth of religions and communities of religious expression other than evangelical Christianity may prove a special challenge for Baptists. Baptists' powerful expression of faith conviction tends to feed a desire to convert and convince others who are different. Until fairly recently, Baptists generally have encountered adherents of other religions—Muslims, Sikhs, Hindus, Buddhists, and others—as subjects for evangelism or objects of mission strategy. As these other faith expressions grow stronger in North America, Baptists will be challenged to find ways to live and work cooperatively with them, as well as to develop nonconfrontational ways of sharing their own faith.

Finally, present world trends and events have led many people to a shift from "religion" to "spirituality" as a way of defining their hunger for meaning. Baptists generally have defined a clear path of confession and commitment focused on a specific understanding of salvation and the exclusive role of Jesus Christ as Savior. Baptists may be challenged to understand their own historical experience of faith development in new ways. Specifically they may have to rediscover the implications of their own principle of soul freedom in order to successfully encounter a generation that frequently and unapologetically draws from pagan sources as well as religious philosophies other than Christianity for religious expression and belief.

These are challenges. They are not, however, prescriptions of doom. Baptists have faced each of these conditions and concerns before, although in different garb. In the end, Baptists have been enlarged and empowered as a result, and there is no reason to doubt that they will be again. There is, in fact, every reason to believe that Baptists will continue to make powerful contributions in the future. The world hungers for faith expression that is based on strong affirmation, personal participation, democratic and inclusive procedures, a vision for a better day, and encouragement for sharing gifts and talents in pursuit of its goals. Baptists have demonstrated these characteristics in abundance from their beginning. They have only to be faithful to the highest and best spirit of their past to assure that they will continue to serve the God who first led them into the waters of their baptism and who has demonstrated the patience to stay with them when the currents were strong.

bibliography

The following list of books is a representative sampling of work by and about Baptists. In a few cases, works noted here describe the circumstances in which Baptists developed rather than Baptists themselves. These works reflect a variety of styles and include volumes written for both scholars and the general public, and they represent older as well as newer works. In some areas of interest, the depth of material available makes choice difficult; in others, it becomes clear that the history of significant segments of Baptist people and their achievements remains to be written. Many of the volumes listed contain significant bibliographies, which in turn will lead the reader to many additional resources. Readers interested in particular subjects or periods may find the American Baptist Historical Society (P.O. Box 851, Valley Forge, PA 19482-0851) of assistance in identifying published works as well as many other materials.

Barnes, Gilbert H. *The Anti-Slavery Impulse, 1830–1844.* New York: Appleton-Century, 1933.

Brackney, William H., ed. *Baptist Life and Thought: 1600–1980.* Valley Forge, Pa.: Judson Press, 1983.

Chernow, Ron. Titan: *The Life of John D. Rockefeller, Sr.* New York: Random House, 1998.

Estep, William R. *Why Baptists? A Study of Baptist Faith and Heritage.* Dallas: Baptist General Convention of Texas, 1997.

Gaustad, Edwin S. *The Great Awakening in New England.* New York: Harper, 1957.

————. *Liberty of Conscience: Roger Williams in America.* Valley Forge, Pa.: Judson Press, 1999.

Gaustad, Edwin S., ed. *Baptists, the Bible, Church Order and the Churches: Essays from* Foundations, *a Baptist Journal of History and Theology.* New York: Arno Press, 1980.

————. *Baptist Piety: The Last Will and Testimony of Obadiah Holmes.* Valley Forge, Pa.: Judson Press, 1994.

Gewehr, Wesley M. *The Great Awakening in Virginia, 1740–1790.* Durham, N.C.: Duke University Press, 1930.

Goen, Clarence C. *Revivalism and Separatism in New England, 1740–1800.* New Haven: Yale University Press, 1962.

Goodwin, Everett C. *The New Hiscox Guide for Baptist Churches.* Valley Forge, Pa.: Judson Press, 1995.

Goodwin, Everett C., ed. *Baptists in the Balance: The Tension between Freedom and Responsibility.* Valley Forge, Pa.: Judson Press, 1997.

Harrison, Paul M. *Authority and Power in the Free Church Tradition: A Social Case Study of the American Baptist Convention.* Princeton, N.J.: Princeton University Press, 1959.

Higginbotham, Evelyn Brooks. *Righteous Discontent: The Women's Movement in the Black Baptist Church, 1880–1920.* Cambridge, Mass.: Harvard University Press, 1993.

Hudson, Winthrop S., ed. *Baptist Concepts of the Church.* Philadelphia.: Judson Press, 1959.

Hodges, Sloan S. *Black Baptists in America and the Origin of Their Conventions.* Washington, D.C.: Progressive National Baptist Convention, 1969.

Lincoln, C. Eric, and Lawrence H. Mamiya. *The Black Church in the African American Experience.* Durham, N.C.: Duke University Press, 1990.

Lumpkin, William L., ed. *Baptist Confessions of Faith.* Philadelphia: Judson Press, 1959.

Maring, Norman H., and Winthrop S. Hudson. *A Baptist Manual of Polity and Practice.* Rev. ed. Valley Forge, Pa.: Judson Press, 1991.

McBeth, Leon. *The Baptist Heritage: Four Centuries of Baptist Witness.* Nashville: Broadman, 1987.

McLoughlin, William G. *Isaac Backus and the American Pietist Tradition.* Boston: 1967.

————. *New England Dissent, 1630–1833: The Baptists and the Separation of Church and State.* 2 vols. Cambridge, Mass.: Harvard University Press, 1971.

————. *Soul Liberty: The Baptist's Struggle in New England, 1630–1833.* Providence: Brown University Press; Hanover, N.H.: University of New England, 1991.

Mild, Warren. *The Story of American Baptists: The Role of a Remnant.* Valley Forge, Pa.: Judson Press, 1976.

Mullins, Edgar Y. *Baptist Beliefs.* 1912. Reprint, Valley Forge, Pa.: Judson Press, 1962.

Paris, Peter J. *The Social Teaching of the Black Churches.* Philadelphia: Fortress, 1985.

Schenkel, Alfred F. *The Rich Man and The Kingdom: John D. Rockefeller, Jr., and the Protestant Establishment.* Minneapolis: Fortress, 1995.

Settle, Mary Lee. *I, Roger Williams.* New York: W. W. Norton & Co., 2001.

Shurden, Walter B. *The Baptist Identity: Four Fragile Freedoms.* Macon, Ga.: Smyth & Helwys, 1993.

Shurden, Walter B., ed. *The Priesthood of All Believers: Proclaiming the Baptist Vision 1.* Macon, Ga.: Smyth & Helwys, 1993.

————. *Religious Liberty: Proclaiming the Baptist Vision 4.* Macon, Ga.: Smyth & Helwys, 1997.

Sobel, Mechal. *Trabelin' On: The Slave Journey to an Afro-Baptist Faith.* Westport, Conn.: Greenwood Press, 1979.

Sweet, William Warren. *The Baptists, 1783–1830.* Vol. 1 of *Religion on the American Frontier.* New York: Henry Holt, 1931.

Taylor, Wilma Rugh, and Norman Thomas Taylor. *This Train Is Bound for Glory: The Story of America's Chapel Cars.* Valley Forge, Pa.: Judson Press, 1999.

Torbet, Robert G. *A History of the Baptists.* 3d ed. Valley Forge, Pa.: Judson Press, 1963.

Vedder, Henry C. *A History of Baptists in the Middle States.* Philadelphia: American Baptist Publication Society, 1898.

Washington, James M. *The Origins and Emergence of Black Baptist Separatism, 1863–1897.* Ann Arbor, Mich.: University Microfilms International, 1980.